PRENTICE HALL
WRITING AND GRAMMAR

Reading Support Practice Book

Grade Nine

Boston, Massachusetts,
Upper Saddle River, New Jersey

ISBN 0-13-361728-9

1 2 3 4 5 6 7 8 9 10   10 09 08 07 06

CONTENTS

NAME _______________________________ **DATE** ___________

Read the following passage. Then answer the questions that follow. Write the letter of the correct answer on the line at the right.

> Utzel got a job as a water carrier. Poverty became a maid. For the first time in their lives, they worked diligently. They were kept so busy they did not even think of the new shoes, until one Sabbath morning Poverty decided she'd try them on again. Lo and behold, her feet slipped easily into them. The new shoes fit.
>
> At last Utzel and Poverty understood that all a man possesses he gains through work, and not by lying in bed and being idle. Even animals were industrious. Bees make honey, spiders spin webs, birds build nests, moles dig holes in the earth, squirrels store food for the winter.

1. Which statement best expresses the main idea of the passage?   1. ______
   - **A.** By working hard, people can earn money for shoes.
   - **B.** The more a person works, the more he or she can possess.
   - **C.** It is possible to profit by being idle.
   - **D.** Only through diligent work do people get what they want.

2. Why did Utzel and Poverty forget about the shoes?   2. ______
   - **A.** They were too tired to think about them.
   - **B.** They were too busy to think about them.
   - **C.** They had learned that shoes were not so important.
   - **D.** Poverty had tried the shoes and they fit.

Read the following passage. Then answer the question that follows. Write the letter of the correct answer on the line at the right.

> The kid had a radio-controlled model army tank, which he used to pursue his dog, a big-boned Irish setter and one of the finest-looking young dogs Cody had ever seen. Sitting on the back steps or in a lawn chair, the kid operated the remote controls and laughed gleefully as the frightened setter fled from the strange, mechanical beast that followed him relentlessly.
>
> At first, the… animal had been able to escape into his doghouse, where the raised entrance had blocked the tank. But then the kid made a ramp with a board, and the next time the setter went in there, the tank went in after him.

3. Which statement expresses the implied main idea of the passage.   3. ______
   - **A.** The setter is one of the best Cody had ever seen.
   - **B.** The kid and the dog are having fun playing together.
   - **C.** The setter is being trained to escape from the tank.
   - **D.** The kid is having fun, but is mistreating the dog.

4. Read the sentence. Then choose the meaning of the underlined word. Write the letter of the correct answer on the line at the right.   4. ______

> Charlie had beaten five out of six challengers in the chess tournament, and he felt <u>indomitable</u>, like a powerful knight.

     A. dumb   **B.** very tired   **C.** unbeatable   **D.** nervous

5. Read the sentence. Then choose the meaning of the underlined word. Write   5. ______
   the letter of the correct answer on the line at the right.

The sixth challenger <u>transformed</u> Charlie's mood into dark gray mush by cornering his king in ten minutes flat.

  A. carried   **B.** changed   **C.** shoved   **D.** flipped

Read the following passage. Then answer the questions that follow. Write the letter of the correct answer on the line at the right.

He came into the room to shut the windows while we were still in bed and I saw he looked ill. He was shivering, his face was white, and he walked slowly as though it ached to move.

"What's the matter, Schatz?"[1]

"I've got a headache."

"You better go back to bed."

"No, I'm all right."

"You go to bed. I'll see you when I'm dressed."

But when I came downstairs, he was dressed, sitting by the fire, looking a very sick and miserable boy of nine years. When I put my hand on his forehead I knew he had a fever.

"You go up to bed," I said, "you're sick."

"I'm all right," he said.

When the doctor came he took the boy's temperature.

"What is it?" I asked him.

"One hundred and two."

Downstairs, the doctor left three different medicines in different colored capsules with instructions for giving them. One was to bring down the fever, another a purgative, the third to overcome an acid condition. The germs of influenza can only exist in an acid condition, he explained. He seemed to know all about influenza and said there was nothing to worry about if the fever did not go above one hundred and four degrees. This was a light epidemic of the flu and there was no danger if you avoided pneumonia.

Back in the room I wrote the boy's temperature down and made a note of the time to give him the various capsules.

---

1. **Schatz** (shats): A German term of affection, used here as a nickname.

6. According to the selection, how did the doctor hope to destroy the influenza germ?   6. ______
   A. by raising the boy's temperature to 104°
   B. by increasing the acid in the boy's body
   C. by avoiding pneumonia
   D. by decreasing the acid in the boy's body

7. Which word sounds exactly like the first syllable in pneu-mo-nia?   7. ______
   A. phew   **B.** new   **C.** pew   **D.** mew

NAME ____ **DATE** _____________

8. What did the doctor do just after he arrived?   8. ______
   A. He left three different medicines.
   B. He told the boy his temperature was too high.
   C. He told the boy's parents to avoid pneumonia.
   D. He took the boy's temperature.

Read the sentences. Then answer the question that follows. Write the letter of the correct answer on the line at the right.

> It was a rough night. Marta's cough was hard enough on her. It also kept six other people awake from sun down right through to sun up.

9. Choose the words in the sentences that rhyme.   9. ______
   A. rough and cough
   B. enough and rough
   C. through and enough
   D. cough and rough

Read the sentence. Then answer the question that follows. Write the letter of the correct answer on the line at the right.

> Greg's father, an architect, often took him along to help inspect the ____________ where a new house would be built.

10. Choose the word that best fills the blank.   10. ______
   A. site   B. sight   C. seat   D. cite

Read the following passage. Then answer the questions that follow. Write the letter of the correct answer on the line at the right.

> The ancients were familiar with five of the planets—Mercury, Venus, Mars, Jupiter, and Saturn—because they are visible to the naked eye. Mercury is quite difficult to see, but the others often shine brilliantly.
>
> There are great differences among the planets. Earth belongs to a group of inner planets, which circle relatively close to the Sun. They are as different from the outer planets as chalk from cheese.
>
> The inner planets are relatively small rocky balls, like the Earth, and they are often called the terrestrial (Earth-like) planets. They contrast markedly with the four giant outer planets Jupiter, Saturn, Uranus, and Neptune. These planets are huge balls of gas. They probably do not have any solid surfaces.
>
> Only Pluto, the tiny fifth outer planet, has not been visited by space probes. It is so distant that it is still as mysterious as ever.

11. Which planets are known as the inner planets?   11. ______
   A. Venus, Earth, Mars, and Jupiter
   B. Mercury, Venus, and Mars
   C. Mercury, Venus, Earth, and Mars
   D. Mercury, Venus, Mars, and Pluto

NAME _______________________________________   DATE _______________

12. Which planets were not known by people in the ancient world?   12. ______
    A. Uranus, Neptune, and Pluto
    B. Mercury, Venus, Mars, Jupiter, and Saturn
    C. Mercury and Pluto
    D. Pluto

13. How are Jupiter, Saturn, Uranus, and Neptune all alike?   13. ______
    A. They are all made of chalk.
    B. They are all the same distance from the Sun.
    C. They all shine brilliantly in the night sky.
    D. They are all giant balls of gas.

14. How are the inner planets different from the four giant outer planets? 14. ______
    A. They do not shine as brilliantly.
    B. They are made up of smaller amounts of gas.
    C. They are much smaller, rocky balls, like Earth.
    D. They all have surface water, unlike the outer planets.

15. Some information in the selection is important and some is unimportant. 15. ______
    Which information is unimportant?
    A. The inner planets are different from the outer planets.
    B. Chalk is different from cheese.
    C. Inner planets circle relatively close to the Sun.
    D. Giant planets probably do not have solid surfaces.

16. How should the word *different* be divided into syllables?   16. ______
    A. diff-er-ent   B. diffe-rent   C. dif-fer-ent   D. dif-fere-nt

17. How should the word *terrestrial* be divided into syllables?   17. ______
    A. ter-res-tri-al   C. terr-est-rial
    B. terra-rest-rial   D. ter-rest-ri-al

Read the sentences. Then answer the questions that follow. Write the letter of the
correct answer on the line at the right.

> She wrote a report about a planet that imports and exports things from other
> planets. A planetary exporter can transport an important portion of the planet's
> portable goods to other planets to support importing an equal proportion of
> other goods.

18. Many words in the selection contain the word root *port*. It comes from the   18. ______
    Latin verb *portare*. What verb best defines the meaning of *port* in these words?
    A. to pour   B. to carry   C. to send   D. to receive

19. What does the prefix *ex-* mean in the word *export*?   19. ______
    A. not or no   B. toward   C. in or into   D. from or out

20. What does the suffix *-er* mean in the word *exporter*?   20. ______
    A. a person who does the action of a verb
    B. more than something else
    C. a person who is female
    D. a person who has license to do something

Read the following passage. Then answer the questions that follow. Write the letter of the correct answer on the line at the right.

> It costs twenty-two cents for a regular stamp now. That's a terrible number, and you don't dare buy a roll of twenty-two cent stamps because you know it's going to change before you get used to it and certainly before you use up a roll.
>
> I object to the fact that it costs me more to send a letter to a friend than it costs some fly-by-night real estate operator to send me a phony brochure in the mail telling me I'm the provisional winner of a $10,000 sweepstakes. I don't like strangers knocking on my door trying to sell me something, and I don't want my mail cluttered with advertising. If anyone wants to accuse me of feeling that way because I make a living from advertising found in newspapers and on television, go ahead and accuse me of it. It isn't true.
>
> I don't get five good, genuine, personal letters a year. The time is coming when the letter written with pen and ink and sent as a personal message from one person to another will be as much of a rarity as the gold pocket watch carried on a chain. It's a shame.

21. Which of the following states an *opinion* about the author's views in the selection?   21. ______
    A. It costs more to mail a personal letter than it costs to mail an advertising brochure.
    B. The author does not like strangers knocking on his door.
    C. The author dislikes sweepstakes.
    D. The author really thinks all advertising by mail is dishonest.

22. Which of the following states a *fact* about the author's views in the selection?   22. ______
    A. The author was probably robbed by a door-to-door salesman.
    B. He or she thinks you have to throw out twenty-two cent stamps if the postage rate goes up.
    C. The author makes a living from newspaper and television advertising.
    D. The author thinks he or she will probably never again receive a handwritten letter.

23. Which of the following best describes the author's purpose in writing the selection?   23. ______
    A. to warn readers about false advertising in the mail
    B. to amuse people with a story about his or her crabby attitudes toward the mail
    C. to say that winning a $10,000 sweepstakes is not worth it
    D. to ask people to write more letters to the author

Read the following passage. Then answer the question that follows. Write the letter of the correct answer on the line at the right.

> So he grew, to become hard, tough, wiry. The muscles on his bones and the cords, tendons, cross weaves of fiber, and nerve centers, these became instruments to obey his wishes. He found with other men he could lift his own end of a log—and more too. One of the neighbors said he was strong as three men. Another said, "He can sink an ax deeper into wood than any man I ever saw." And another, "If you heard him fellin' trees in a clearin', you would say there was three men at work by the way the trees fell."

24. Which of the following best describes the author's point of view toward the person he or she is writing about? 24. ______
    A. The author disapproves of him for cutting down so many trees.
    B. The author admires him as a remarkable, promising young man.
    C. The author admires his strength, but thinks he may use it unwisely.
    D. The author disapproves of him for being a show off.

Read the following passage. Then answer the question that follows. Write the letter of the correct answer on the line at the right.

> She looked straight into my eyes, as if she could see all the things that were muddling around inside my brain.
>
> "Rinko, don't ever be ashamed of who you are." she said. "Just be the best person you can. Believe in your own worth. And someday I know you'll be able to feel proud of yourself, even the part of you that's different… the part that's Japanese."
>
> I was still in my slip sitting next to Aunt Waka and wriggling my toes as I listened to her. And then it happened, like a light bulb had been switched on in my head. At that very minute I finally knew what made Aunt Waka seem so special. She was exactly the kind of person she was telling me to be. She believed in herself and she liked herself. But mostly, I guess she was proud of who she was.

25. Which of the following best describes what was troubling Rinko? 25. ______
    A. She is troubled about feeling different because she is Japanese.
    B. She is troubled because her Aunt Waka is so different from other people.
    C. She is troubled because Aunt Waka wants her to feel proud.
    D. She is troubled because no one notices that she is Japanese.

Use the chart below to answer the following questions.

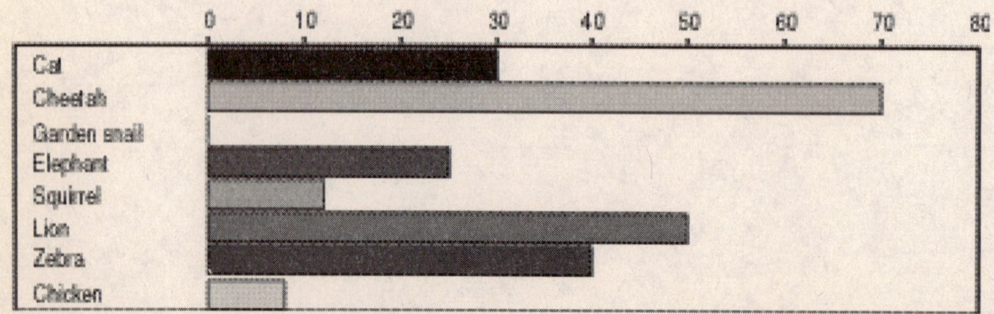

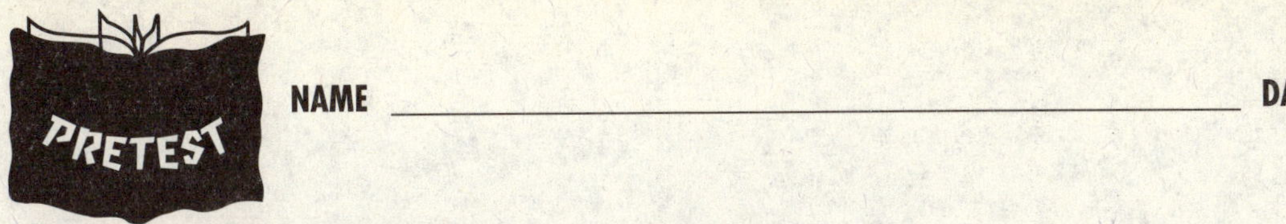

26. Which animal on the chart moves slowest?   26. _______
    A. elephant   **C.** chicken
    B. cheetah   **D.** garden snail

27. According to the chart, how fast does a squirrel move?   27. _______
    A. 50 miles per hour   **C.** 12 miles per hour
    B. 9 miles per hour   **D.** 15 miles per hour

Read the following passage. Then answer the question that follows. Write the letter of the correct answer on the line at the right.

> The first thing to understand about poetry is that it comes to you from outside you, in books or in words, but that for it to live, something from within you must come to it and meet it and complete it. Your response with your own mind and body and memory and emotions gives the poem its ability to work its magic; if you give to it, it will give to you, and give plenty.
>
> When you read, don't let the poet write down to you; read up to him. Reach for him from your gut out, and the heart and muscles will come into it, too.

28. Which of the following statements best summarizes the passage?   28. _______
    A. Most poetry is not very rewarding.
    B. Poetry lives only on the written page.
    C. If you give to poetry, it will give to you.
    D. Poetry comes to you from outside you.

Read the following passage. Then answer the question that follows. Write the letter of the correct answer on the line at the right.

> Hong Kong poses a different problem to someone learning to speak Chinese. The native dialect of most residents of Hong Kong is Cantonese, a dialect that cannot be understood by native speakers of the Mandarin dialect. Mandarin is becoming more and more popular in Hong Kong with the approach of the year 1997, when the British will return Hong Kong to China. But because English is a widely spoken second language in Hong Kong, an English speaking visitor should be able to get by with little difficulty.

29. Choose the statement that is the best generalization about the languages   29. _______
    spoken in Hong Kong.
    A. Mandarin and Cantonese are the main languages.
    B. Mandarin is replacing English as the main language.
    C. English may be more useful than Mandarin in Hong Kong.
    D. Learning Mandarin will not help you understand Cantonese

Read the following passages and answer the questions that follow. Write the letter of the correct answer on the line at the right.

> Now, with supper finished, we retire to the room in a faraway part of the house where my friend sleeps in a scrap-quilt-covered iron bed painted rose pink, her favorite color. Silently, wallowing in the pleasures of conspiracy, we take the bead purse from its secret place and spill its contents on the scrap quilt.

30. Which statement below paraphrases the first sentence of the passage above?   30. ______
    A. We can't go to my friend's room until we finish supper.
    B. After supper, we went to my friend's room and spilled the contents of a bead purse on her scrap-quilt-covered iron bed.
    C. After supper, we went to a faraway room in the house where my friend sleeps in a quilt-covered iron bed that is painted in her favorite color, rose pink.
    D. Now, with supper finished, we retire to the room in a faraway part of the house where my friend sleeps in a scrap-quilt-covered iron bed painted in rose pink, her favorite color.

> Cats have fabulous memories, I maintain, and also the ability to measure and evaluate what they remember.

31. Which statement below is a paraphrase of the sentence above?   31. ______
    A. I think cats remember everything that humans forget.
    B. Cats have many happy memories.
    C. Cats have fabulous memories, I maintain, and also the ability to measure and evaluate what they remember.
    D. I think cats have excellent memories and are able to measure and make judgments about what they remember.

Read the following passage. Then answer the question that follows. Write the letter of the correct answer on the line at the right.

> "Can I ask you a question?" Julio asked the old man.
>
> "Man, I don't get you. You got a whole apartment next door all to yourself—six rooms! And you gotta come here to eat in this crowded kitchen. Why?"
>
> "First of all, today is Saturday, and I thought I could bring in my food and your mama could turn on the stove for me. You know, in my religion you can't light a fire on Saturday."
>
> "You come here anytime; I turn on the stove for you, don't worry," Mrs. Suárez said.
>
> "Man, what about other days? We been living here for about six months, right?" Julio persisted. "And you do more cooking here than in your own place."

32. According to the selection, what can be inferred about the old man?   32. ______
    A. The old man does not like to cook in his own apartment.
    B. The old man is lonely.
    C. The old man is poor and does not have any food at home.
    D. The old man is very religious.

Read the passage below and then answer the question that follows. Write the letter of the correct answer on the line at the right.

> Besides history, geography, and arithmetic, Miss Kinnian said I should start to learn foreign languages. Dr. Strauss gave me some more tapes to play while I sleep. I still don't understand how the conscious and unconscious mind works, but Dr. Strauss says not to worry yet. He asked me to promise that when I start college subjects next week I wouldn't read any books on psychology—that is, until he gives me permission.

33. Which word sounds exactly like the first syllable in *psy-chol-o-gy?*   33. _______
    A. pie   **C.** sigh
    B. see   **D.** shy

Read the following passage. Then answer the question that follows. Write the letter of the correct answer on the line at the right.

> His room was as black as pitch with the thick darkness (for the shutters were close fastened, through fear of robbers), and so I knew that he could not see the opening of the door, and I kept pushing on it steadily, steadily.
>
> I had my head in, and was about to open the lantern, when my thumb slipped upon the tin fastening, and the old man sprang up in bed, crying out—"Who's there?"
>
> I kept quite still and said nothing. For a whole hour I did not move a muscle, and in the meantime I did not hear him lie down. He was still sitting up in the bed listening—just as I have done, night after night, hearkening to the death watches,[1] in the wall.
>
> ______
> **1. death watches:** Small beetles that live in wood and make a ticking sound.

34. What did the narrator do just after he heard the old man cry out?   34. _______
    A. He pushed the door open.
    B. He kept still for an hour.
    C. He listened to the death watches in the wall.
    D. He was about to open the lantern.

Read the passage below and then answer the question that follows. Write the letter of the correct answer on the line at the right.

> She heated some lima beans and ham, made the cocoa, and set the table. The woman did not ask the boy anything about where he lived, or his folks, or anything else that would embarrass him. Instead, as they ate, she told him about her job in a hotel beauty shop, what the work was like, and how all kinds of women came in and out. Then she cut him half of her ten-cent cake.
>
> "Eat some more, son," she said.
>
> When they finished eating, she got up and said, "Now here, take these ten dollars and buy yourself some suede shoes. And, next time, do not make the mistake of latching onto my pocketbook nor nobody *else's*—because shoes got by devilish ways will burn your feet. I got to get my rest now. But from here on in, son, I hope you will behave yourself."

35. Some information in the selection is important and some is not important.   35. ______
    Which information is unimportant?
    A. She wanted him to eat more.
    B. She cut him half of her ten-cent cake.
    C. She did not ask him embarrassing questions.
    D. She gave him money to buy shoes.

Read the sentences below and answer the questions that follow. Write the letter of
the correct answer on the line at the right.

> In our nightly discussions around the fire, our conversation narrowed more and
> more to the immediate problems confronting us, and during them I began to
> realize that the tension between Osborn and Nace went deeper than I had surmised.

36. The word *confronting* contains the word root *front,* which comes from the Latin   36. ______
    fróns. What word below best defines the meaning of *confronting*?
    A. for something
    B. facing
    C. in back of
    D. to blend with

37. "'You're a geologist, Frank,' he began without preamble." What do you think   37. ______
    the prefix *pre-* means in the word *preamble*?
    A. against
    B. knowing of
    C. ending
    D. before

38. What do you think the suffix *-amble* means in the same word?   38. ______
    A. get in front of
    B. hesitation
    C. walk
    D. knowledge

Read the following passage. Then answer the question that follows. Write the letter
of the correct answer on the line at the right.

> How come kitty acts not like the beast of prey she is but like a better-class human
> being? I don't know the answer. The point is, she does it—and it makes you her
> slave ever after. Once you have been presented with a mouse by your cat, you
> will never be the same again. She can use you for a door mat. And she will, too.

39. Which would be the best conclusion about how the author feels about cats?   39. ______
    A. A cat is better than a human being.
    B. A cat rules its owner.
    C. A dog is more friendly.
    D. Cats give mice to their owners.

Read the following passage. Then answer the question that follows. Write the letter of the correct answer on the line at the right.

> My grandmother. My poor, poor grandmother. Old people aren't supposed to have those kinds of memories. You see their pictures in the family albums and that's what they are: pictures. They're not supposed to come to life. You drive out in your father's Le Mans doing seventy-five on the pike and all you're doing is visiting an old lady in a nursing home. A duty call. And then you find out that she's a person. She's *somebody*. She's my grandmother, all right, but she's also herself, like my own mother and father. They exist outside of their relationship to me. I was scared again. I wanted to get out of there.

40. Which of the following statements best summarizes the passage?   40. ______
   A. Visiting a grandmother in a nursing home is a duty.
   B. It's boring to look at old pictures in a family album.
   C. A grandmother is her own person.
   D. Old people lose their memories.

Read the following passage. Then answer the question that follows. Write the letter of the correct answer on the line at the right.

> The person to whom she is speaking is myself. I am seven; she is sixty-something. We are cousins, very distant ones, and we have lived together—well, as long as I can remember. Other people inhabit the house, relatives; and though they may have power over us, and frequently make us cry, we are not, on the whole, too much aware of them. We are each other's best friend. She calls me Buddy, in memory of a boy who was formerly her best friend. The other Buddy died in the 1880's, when she was still a child. She is still a child.

41. Which statement is the best generalization about the two cousins?   41. ______
   A. They live in the same house.
   B. Buddy and his cousin are the best of friends.
   C. Buddy's cousin once had a best friend also named Buddy.
   D. Buddy and his cousin cry a lot.

Read the following passage. Then answer the question that follows. Write the letter of the correct answer on the line at the right.

> Did you ever try to keep a cat out that wanted to come in, or vice versa? I once locked a cat in the cellar. He climbed a straight, smooth cement wall, hung on with his paws (I saw the claw marks to prove it); unfastened the window hook with his nose, and climbed out.

42. Which statement best expresses the implied main idea of the passage?   42. ______
   A. It is all right to lock a cat in the cellar.
   B. Cats often unlock window hooks and get out of cellars.
   C. Cats are very smart and very determined.
   D. Cats are able to do whatever they please.

DECODING: TRICKY LETTER COMBINATIONS

Introduction

When you come across unfamiliar words in your reading, try pronouncing the words. Think about the way each sound is spelled. Notice any unusual spellings. You may find that some of the words do not sound the way they are spelled.

Note the difference between the spelling and pronunciation of the word *caught.* The letters *g* and *h* are silent. Think about other words you know that are similar in spelling to *caught.*

Suppose a passage that you are reading contains the word *haughty.* You can use what you know about the *augh* letter combination in other words to figure out how to pronounce *haughty,* which means "proud."

In words with the letter combinations *igh* and *ought, gh is* also silent, as it is in the *augh* combination. Study the examples below. (Notice that the vowel sounds in words with the *ought* combination sometimes differ.)

Words with the *igh* combination	Words with the *ought* combination
night	fought
right	drought
sigh	

Now consider the difference between the spelling and pronunciation of the word *should.* In the *ould* combination, the *l* is silent. Think about other words you know that are similar in spelling to *should.*

Reading Tip
Many English words do not sound the way they are spelled. Use what you already know about words with tricky letter combinations to help you figure out the pronunciations of words that have similar combinations.

NAME ____   DATE _____________

Practice

Read the following passage from "The Finish of Patsy Barnes," a short story by Paul Laurence Dunbar.

> Patsy was incorrigible. Even into the confines of Little Africa had penetrated the truant officer and the terrible penalty of the compulsory education law. Time and time again had poor Eliza Barnes been brought up on account of the shortcomings of that son of hers. She was a hard-working, honest woman, and day by day bent over her tub, scrubbing away to keep Patsy in shoes and jackets, that would wear out so much faster than they could be bought. But she never murmured, for she loved the boy with a deep affection, though his misdeeds were a sore thorn in her side.
>
> She wanted him to go to school. She wanted him to learn. She had the notion that he might become something better, something higher than she had been. But for him school had no charms; his school was the cool stalls in the big livery stable near at hand; the arena of his pursuits its sawdust floor; the height of his ambition, to be a horseman. Either here or in the racing stables at the Fair-grounds he spent his truant hours. It was a school that taught much, and Patsy was as apt a pupil as he was a constant attendant. He learned strange things about horses, and fine, sonorous oaths that sounded eerie on his young lips, for he had only turned into his fourteenth year.

A. Identify words in the passage that have the letter combinations shown below. Write the words below each heading. Say each word aloud. Then write its meaning next to it. If necessary, look it up in the dictionary.

augh	igh	ought	ould

B. Challenge!

In the *ough* letter combination at the end of words, the *gh* can be silent, or it can have the /f/ sound. Write at least one example of each case below.

1. *ough,* in which *gh* is silent ____

2. *ough,* in which *gh* has the /f/ sound: _________________________________

DECODING: SOUND/LETTER PATTERNS

Introduction

As you explore word meaning and pronunciation in your reading, you may have noticed that certain letter patterns produce specific sounds. For example, in the *tion* pattern at the end of a word, *ti* has the sound /sh/, as in *friction* and *correction*.

Words that end with the /shən/ sound are usually spelled with the *-tion* ending. In some cases, this sound can be spelled *-sion,* as in *tension* and *propulsion,* usually when a consonant comes before the /shən/ ending.

Most words that end in a vowel plus *sion* have the /zhən/ sound, as in *decision* and *vision.*

You may have also noticed in your reading that words with more than one syllable whose last, unaccented syllable ends in *-ar, -er,* and *-or* have the same ending sound, /ər/. Examples are *hangar, offer,* and *monitor.* The /ər/ sound does not change when *-s, -ed,* and *-ing* are added to a base word that ends in *-ar, -er,* and *-or,* as in *hangars, offered,* and *monitoring.*

Another pattern you may have noticed is the /f/ sound produced by *ph* in words that you read. The sound /f/ can be produced by the letter pattern *ph* at the beginning, in the middle, and at the end of words. Note the examples below.

- /f/ sound made by *ph* pattern at the beginning of a word: photograph, phrase, physician
- /f/ sound made by *ph* pattern in the middle of a word: gopher, emphasize, telephone
- /f/ sound made by *ph* pattern at the end of a word: graph, hieroglyph

Reading Tip

When you discover an unfamiliar word in your reading, first try pronouncing the word. Think about the way each sound is spelled. Look for sound/letter patterns that you are familiar with, such as *tion/sion, ar/er/or,* and *ph.* Apply what you already know about sound/letter patterns to the new word. Once you are able to pronounce a word, you may discover that you are familiar with it even though it may have seemed unfamiliar when you first saw it.

Practice

Read the following passage from "The Open Window," a short story by Saki.

"The doctors agree in ordering me complete rest, an absence of mental excitement, and avoidance of anything in the nature of violent physical exercise," announced Framton, who labored under the tolerably widespread delusion that total strangers and chance acquaintances are hungry for the least detail of one's ailments and infirmities, their cause and cure. "On the matter of diet they are not so much in agreement," he continued.

"No?" said Mrs. Sappleton, in a voice which only replaced a yawn at the last moment. Then she suddenly brightened into alert attention—but not to what Framton was saying.

"Here they are at last!" she cried. "Just in time for tea, and don't they look as if they were muddy up to the eyes!"

Framton shivered slightly and turned towards the niece with a look intended to convey sympathetic comprehension. The child was staring out through the open window with dazed horror in her eyes. In a chill shock of nameless fear, Framton swung round in his seat and looked in the same direction.

In the deepening twilight three figures were walking across the lawn towards the window; they all carried guns under their arms, and one of them was additionally burdened with a white coat hung over his shoulders. A tired brown spaniel kept close at their heels. Noiselessly they neared the house, and then a hoarse young voice chanted out of the dusk: "I said, Bertie, why do you bound?"

Identify words in the passage that have the sound/letter patterns shown below. Write the words below each heading.

Words that end with *sion/tion*	Words that have *ar/er/or* as the second, unaccented syllable (can include *s*, *ed*, and *ing* endings)	Words in which *ph* stands for the /f/ sound

Pronounce each word aloud. Which of these words do you use in your everyday speech? What is the meaning of these words?

____

____

DECODING: SYLLABICATION

Introduction

A **syllable** is a unit of language: it can be a word or part of a word. Each syllable in a word has one vowel sound. As you explore word pronunciation and meaning during your reading, it is sometimes helpful to divide a word into its syllables. Often, one or more of the syllables is an important clue to meaning. In addition, when you say the word aloud, you may realize that it's one you already use in your everyday speech— and you may not have recognized it by just seeing it on the page. To divide a word into syllables, first listen for the vowel sounds.

Pronounce the words *beat* and *create*. Notice that in *beat,* the letters *e* and *a* together have one vowel sound and one syllable. In *create,* the letters *e* and *a* make two different vowel sounds. *Create* has two syllables: cre • ate.

Use these rules to help you divide words into syllables:

1. If a word has two vowel sounds between two consonant letters, divide the word between the two vowels.

   ruin   ru • in
   trial   tri • al
   react   re • act

2. If a word has two consonants between two vowels, divide the word between the two consonants.

   injure   in • jure
   letter   let • ter
   import   im • port

3. If a word has two of the same consonants next to each other, divide the word between the two consonants.

   common   com • mon
   effect   ef • fect
   approve   ap • prove

4. If a word has a middle consonant between two vowels, listen for the accented syllable in the word. The middle consonant is part of the accented syllable.

   pretend   pre • tend'
   melon   mel' • on
   salute   sa • lute'

Reading Tip
Remember to listen for the vowel sounds when you divide a word into syllables.

Practice

Read the following passage about the painter Wang Yani from "A Young Painter," by Zheng Zhensun and Alice Low.

Wang Yani was born and grew up in the small town of Gongcheng, which is in the Guangxi Zhuang Autonomous Region of southern China. This is a beautiful area with green hills, clear blue rivers, and ancient temples. Not far away are the famous cone-shaped, rugged mountains of Guilin, which have an unreal, fairy-tale quality, especially when they are shrouded in mist and clouds.

Next door to Yani's home in Gongcheng was a Confucian temple where lovely flowers bloomed. In front of the house there was a lotus pond, and Chaijiang River, full of fish, flowed nearby. Yani and her younger brother, Wang Xiangyu, often played by the river. They floated boats in it, waded across it, or went rafting. Yani liked to take a stroll along the riverbank every day.

A. List twelve words from the passage that have two syllables. (Do not list proper nouns—words that begin with capital letters.) Say each word aloud to decide how many syllables it has. Draw a line between the syllables of each word.

_______________   _______________   _______________

_______________   _______________   _______________

_______________   _______________   _______________

_______________   _______________   _______________

B. Challenge!

With a partner, go through one or two of the selections in your literature book to find at least two more examples of words following each of the rules on the previous page. Then think of words you both use in your everyday speech, and come up with at least one more example for each of the rules. Finally, look through your list and circle any syllables that can stand by themselves as words. Look up the meaning of each of those syllables. Then explain how the syllable contributes to the overall meaning of the word.

NAME _______________________________ DATE _________

RECOGNIZING WORD ROOTS

Introduction

In the English language, many words have a "core" section, or root. Consider, for example, the word *prehistorically*. *Pre* and *ic* and *ally* attach to the root, *histor*, which means "knowing" in Greek.

Some common roots include *sad* in *sadness*, *happy* in *unhappiness*, and *warn* in *forewarned*. You might say that roots are the building blocks of our language. Roots are an important reading and vocabulary tool, because they can help you figure out the meaning of words that are unfamiliar. Read the passage below from "The Masque of the Red Death," by Edgar Allan Poe. Look for other word roots.

> But the Prince Prospero was happy and dauntless and sagacious. When his dominions were half depopulated, he summoned to his presence a thousand hale and lighthearted friends from among the knights and dames of his court, and with these retired to the deep seclusion of one of his castellated abbeys.[1] This was an extensive and magnificent structure, the creation of the prince's own eccentric yet august[2] taste. A strong and lofty wall girdled it in. This wall had gates of iron. The courtiers, having entered, brought furnaces and massy[3] hammers and welded the bolts.

1. **castellated abbeys:** Monasteries or convents with castlelike towers.
2. **august:** Distinguished or regal, kinglike.
3. **massy:** Massive or large.

There are several roots in the above passage. For example, notice the word *depopulated*. When you encounter an unfamiliar word like *depopulated* in your reading, see if the word contains a familiar root. In this case, the root of *depopulated* is *populate*, which means "to supply with people or inhabitants." When you see that root together with the prefix *de-*, which means "to make the opposite of," you can infer that the word *depopulate* means "to reduce the people or inhabitants of" a place. On the chart below, you will see how three words from the passage—*depopulated*, *castellated*, and *courtiers*—are formed from word roots. Notice that *castellated is* formed from the root *castle* and the suffix *-ate*, meaning "resembling," and that *courtiers* is formed from the root *court* and the suffix *-ier*, meaning "one associated with."

Word	Root	Meaning of Root	Meaning of Word
depopulated	populate	to supply with inhabitants	sharply reduce the inhabitants of a place
castellated	castle	a fortified stronghold	furnished with turrets and battlements in the style of a castle
courtiers	court	residence of a sovereign	attendants at the court of a sovereign

Practice

Below, you'll find another passage from "The Masque of the Red Death."
Please read the passage. As you read, look for words in the passage that
have been formed from the roots that are listed in the chart below. Write
these larger words in the first column of the chart. Then write the
meaning of the root, and think about how knowing the root's meaning
can help you understand the meaning of the larger word. Write the
meaning of the word in the last column of the chart.

> …It was then, however, that the Prince Prospero, maddening with rage
> and the shame of his own momentary cowardice, rushed hurriedly
> through the six chambers, while none followed him on account of a
> deadly terror that had seized upon all. He bore aloft a drawn dagger, and
> had approached, in rapid impetuosity,[4] to within three or four feet of
> the retreating figure, when the latter, having attained the extremity[5] of
> the velvet apartment, turned suddenly and confronted his pursuer.

4. impetuosity: Impulsive behavior.
5. extremity: Furthest point or end.

	Word	Root	Meaning of Root	Meaning of Word
1.		mad		
2.		moment		
3.		coward		
4.		hurry		
5.		dead		
6.		impetuous		
7.		extreme		
8.		part		
9.		sudden		
10.		pursue		

PREFIXES/SUFFIXES

Introduction

A **prefix** is a letter or letters attached to the front of a word or root to create a new word (for example, *dis*agree, *pre*caution, *be*little). A **suffix** is a letter or letters attached to the end of a word or root to create a new word (for example, fear*ful*, ador*able*). By adding prefixes and suffixes to existing words, you can vastly expand your vocabulary. Learning the meaning of prefixes and suffixes will also help you to piece together the meanings of some unfamiliar words.

While you are reading, you can often figure out a word you don't know by breaking it down into its parts. For example, suppose you come across the word *unkindness* in your reading. You can decode the word by breaking it down into three parts (*un-kind-ness*):

1. *un-*, a prefix meaning "not" or "the opposite of"
2. *kind*, a word meaning "showing concern and sympathy for others"
3. *-ness*, a suffix meaning "a state, quality, or condition"

When you look at the word parts, you realize that *unkindness* means "the state of lacking sympathy and concern for others."

The chart below lists several common prefixes and suffixes and explains what they mean. Study the chart so you can recall these meanings when you are reading a textbook or story. Knowledge of prefixes and suffixes will save you a lot of time when you are trying to decode words as you read.

Prefix	Meaning	Suffix	Meaning
be-	completely, excessively	*-er*	one that performs a certain task
circum-	around, about	*-est*	the most, forms the superlative degree
dis-	not	*-graph*	something written or drawn
in-	not or in, into, within	*-ly*	in the manner of
pre-	before, prior to	*-ment*	action, process
un-	opposite of	*-ness*	state, quality, degree
re-	again, anew	*-ology*	science, study
non-	not	*-ty*	condition, quality

Practice

As you read the passage below from "A Visit to Grandmother," by
William Melvin Kelley, suppose that you don't know the meanings of the
words *warmest, timidly, uncertainty,* and *sadness.* These words are listed on
the chart below the passage. On the chart, write any prefix or suffix
contained in these words and what the prefix or suffix means. Then
figure out the meaning of each word, and write that meaning in the last
column of the chart.

> Chig knew something was wrong the instant his father kissed her. He
> had always known his father to be the warmest of men, a man so kind
> that when people ventured timidly into his office, it took only a few
> words from him to make them relax, and even laugh. Doctor Charles
> Dunford cared about people.
>
> But when he had bent to kiss the old lady's black face, something new
> and almost ugly had come into his eyes: fear, uncertainty, sadness, and
> perhaps even hatred.

Word	Prefix	Suffix	Root	Meaning
1. warmest			warm, "loving"	
2. timidly			timid, "fearful," "hesitant"	
3. uncertainty			certain, "sure" "confident"	
4. sadness			sad, "affected by sorrow"	

INFLECTED FORMS: PLURALS AND TENSES

Introduction

An **inflection** is a sound that is added to the end of a word. It changes the word's meaning in some way. Compare the two words *fox* and *foxes*. The sound /iz/ has been added to the stem word *fox*, and changes its meaning from singular to plural. "Foxes" is what is called an **inflected form.** The *-es* is the inflection, a special kind of suffix. In English, the sound of the inflections *-s, -es,* or *-ies* is used to change many singular nouns to plural nouns.

Inflections are also used to change the tense of verbs. For example, *endanger* and *endangered*. Notice how the addition on the sound /ed/ changes this verb from the present to the past tense.

There are other uses of inflections in English, but these are two of the most important. Understanding how inflections are used will increase your understanding of grammar and help you be a better writer.

Read the passage below from "Crime on Mars," by Arthur C. Clarke. Notice that the verbs *continued, replied, taken, checked, wondered,* and *tries* are all inflected forms.

> "At the same time," continued the Inspector, "now and then there's a case that makes life interesting. You're an art dealer, Mr. Maccar; I'm sure you heard about that spot of bother at Meridian City a couple of months ago."
>
> "I don't think so," replied the plump, olive-skinned little man I'd taken for just another returning tourist. Presumably the Inspector had already checked through the passenger list; I wondered how much he knew about me, and tried to reassure myself that my conscience was—well—reasonably clear. After all, everybody took *something* out through Martian Customs.

The stems of the inflected verbs are *continue, reply, take, check, wonder,* and *try.* The inflected forms let you know that all of the action takes place in the past. The narrator is telling the reader about it. Inflections are also important in subject-verb agreement. For example, in the present tense you would say "continues the Inspector," not "continued the Inspector." Notice that the *-s* inflection is used here. This is the same sound used to change some singular nouns to plurals.

Practice

Below, the passage from "Crime on Mars" continues. Read the passage carefully, and watch for both plural and tense inflections. *(Hint:* Watch for plural nouns and for verbs in the past tense.)

"It's been rather well hushed up," said the Inspector, "but you can't keep these things quiet for long. Anyway, a jewel thief from Earth tried to steal Meridian Museum's greatest treasure—the Siren Goddess."

"But that's absurd!" I objected. "It's priceless, of course—but it's only a lump of sandstone. You couldn't sell it to anyone—you might just as well steal the Mona Lisa."

The inspector grinned, rather mirthlessly. *"That's* happened once," he said. "Maybe the motive was the same. There are collectors who would give a fortune for such an object, even if they could only look at it themselves. Don't you agree, Mr. Maccar?"

A. List two inflected nouns from the passage above. How does the inflection change their meaning?

____

____

B. List five inflected verbs from the passage above. List those with /ed/ sound endings in one list and those with the /t/ sound endings in another. How do the inflections change the meaning of the verbs?

____

____

____

____

____

CONTEXT CLUES

Introduction

When you read an unfamiliar word, you can use **context clues** to figure out its meaning. Context clues are clues in the text surrounding a word. Look for context clues in the sentence that contains the unfamiliar word or in the phrases and sentences nearby.

Model 1

The following passage is from "The Rap on the Door," by Robert Fulghum. In the underlined part of the sentence, Fulghum compares a boy's expression with the face of a pilot. Notice how this comparison might help readers define the word *intently*.

> <u>Like a pilot in a fog relying on limited instruments</u>, the boy looks **intently** at my face for information.

Unfamiliar Word	Context Clues	Definition
intently	Like a pilot in a fog relying on limited instruments	with great concentration

Model 2

Fulghum uses the word *matronly* in the following passage. Study the underlined phrases to find context clues that help define the word. As you read the passage, create a definition for the word *matronly* in your mind. Then compare your definition with the one in the chart below.

> Across the back of our house is a row of <u>middle-aged</u> **matronly** maple trees, <u>extravagantly dressed</u> in season in a million leaf-sequins. And in season the sequins detach. Not much wind in our sheltered yard, so the leaves lie about the <u>ladies'</u> feet now like <u>dressing gowns</u> they've stepped out of in preparation for the bath of winter.

Unfamiliar Word	Context Clues	Definition
matronly	middle-aged, extravagantly dressed, ladies', dressing gowns	having the qualities of a mature woman who has an established place in society

NAME ____ **DATE** ___________

Practice

Part I

Below is another passage from "The Rap on the Door," by Robert Fulghum. Read the passage and then complete the chart.

> In a way, the trees are there because of the leaves. With unbridled extravagance, zillions of seeds have helicoptered out of the sky to land like assault forces to green the earth. The leaves follow to cover, protect, warm, and nourish the next generation of trees. Stony ground, rot, mold, bacteria, birds, squirrels, bugs, and people—all <u>intervene</u>. But somehow, some make it. Some <u>tenacious</u> seeds take hold and hold on and hold on—for dear life. In the silence of winter's dark they <u>prevail</u> and plant themselves and survive to become the next generation of trees. It has been thus for eons, and we mess with the process at our peril, say I. This is important.

Unfamiliar Word	Context Clues	Definition
intervene		
tenacious		
prevail		

Part II

The following passage is from "The Most Dangerous Game," by Richard
Connell. As you read the passage, circle the context clues that might help
you define the underlined words. Then complete the chart on the next page.

> There was no sound in the night as Rainsford sat there, but the muffled
> throb of the engine that drove the yacht swiftly through the darkness,
> and the swish and ripple of the wash of the propeller.
>
> Rainsford, reclining in a steamer chair, <u>indolently</u> puffed on his favorite
> <u>brier</u>. The sensuous drowsiness of the night was on him. "It's so dark,"
> he thought, "that I could sleep without closing my eyes; the night would
> be my eyelids—"
>
> An abrupt sound startled him. Off to the right he heard it, and his ears,
> expert in such matters, could not be mistaken. Again he heard the sound,
> and again. Somewhere off in the blackness, someone had fired a gun
> three times.
>
> Rainsford sprang up and moved quickly to the rail, mystified. He
> strained his eyes in the direction from which the <u>reports</u> had come, but
> it was like trying to see through a blanket. He leaped upon the rail and
> balanced himself there, to get greater elevation; his pipe, striking a rope,
> was knocked from his mouth. He <u>lunged</u> for it; a short, hoarse cry came
> from his lips as he realized he had reached too far and had lost his balance.
> The cry was pinched off short as the blood-warm waters of the Caribbean
> Sea closed over his head.

NAME _________________________________ DATE _________

Part II (continued)

Unfamiliar Word	Context Clues	Definition
indolently		
brier		
reports		
lunged		

NAME _________________________ DATE __________

ACTIVE READING: SET A PURPOSE

Introduction

Different types of writing present different reasons for reading. For example, we read textbooks, for a different reason than we might read magazines. When reading a textbook, you might skim for information to prepare for a test. When reading a magazine, you might read quickly and for entertainment. Before sitting down to read, you might want to set a purpose for reading.

Setting a purpose for reading involves identifying specific questions that you will answer during reading. By asking yourself specific questions before you begin, you direct your attention to the key ideas in the passage. You can get an idea of what the selection is about by looking at the:

- title
- subheadings
- illustrations

You might also want to read the first sentence or passage for further information. Use three steps to help you set a purpose:

Setting a Purpose

1. Study the title and illustrations.
2. Read the first sentence or paragraph.
3. Look for clues in the text (is the writing informative or entertainment?)

Model

Read the following beginning of a passage from "The Loch Ness Monster," by John McPhee. Think of your own questions that you could use to get a purpose for reading this passage. Then compare your questions to the ones below.

> My children had watched, some months earlier, the killing of a small snake on a lawn in Maryland. About eighteen inches long, it came out from a basement-window well, through a covering lattice of redwood, and was noticed with shouts and shrieks by the children and a young retriever that barked at the snake and leaped about in a circle.

Questions

Why would you read this passage? What information might you expect to find?

Purpose for Reading

- To find out how and why the snake was killed
- To learn about the snake's effect on the children

NAME _______________________________   **DATE** _____________

Practice

Read the following passage from "The Loch Ness Monster," by John McPhee, and answer the questions below.

…In every sense except possibly the sense that involves cruelty, the creature in Loch Ness is indeed a monster. An average taken from many films and sightings gives its mature length at about forty feet. Its general appearance is repulsive, in the instant and radical sense in which reptiles are repulsive to many human beings, and any number of people might find difficulty in accepting a creature that looks like the one that was slain by St. George. Its neck, about six feet long, columnar, powerfully muscled, is the neck of a serpent. Its head, scarcely broader than the neck, is a serpent's head, with uncompromising, lenticular eyes. Sometimes as it swims it holds its head and neck erect. The creature's mouth is at least a foot wide. Its body undulates. Its skin glistens when wet and appears coarse, mottled, gray, and stretches back to something of a point. It seemed to me, sitting there at Headquarters, that the classical mythical, dragon likeness of this animate thing—the modified dinosaur, the fantastically exaggerated newt—was an impediment to the work of the investigation bureau, which has no pertinent interest in what the monster resembles or calls to mind but a great deal in what it actually is, the goal being a final and positive identification of the genus.

A. Answer the following questions.

1. What do you think might be the purpose or purposes for reading the passage? Why? ____

2. List at least ten details you learned about the Loch Ness Monster from reading this passage.

1. _______________________   6. _______________________

2. _______________________   7. _______________________

3. _______________________   8. _______________________

4. _______________________   9. _______________________

5. _______________________   10. ______________________

B. Challenge!

List three different kinds of books or written materials you might read on your own and your purpose for reading them.

Type of Book	Purpose for Reading
1.	
2.	
3.	

ACTIVE READING: PREDICT

Introduction

When you use what you *know* to explain what you *think is* going to happen, you are making a **prediction.** Predictions are based on two factors:
- information from the story
- knowledge from your own personal experience

Making predictions can make reading more exciting because you become actively involved with what you are reading.

Making Predictions: Three Steps

Step 1

Ask yourself what you know about the story and the characters so far; look for descriptions and clues in the text and make notes to yourself about those clues and details.

Step 2

Ask yourself what your own personal experiences have taught you about the details you wrote in your notes.

Step 3

Based on what you discovered in steps 1 and 2, ask yourself what you think will happen. Write your predictions down on a piece of paper.

Reading Tip

To help you make predictions in your reading, think about other stories and books you have read.
- What predictions did you make?
- Was the story different from your expectations? If so, how?
- What surprised you about the story if anything?
- Were your predictions correct?

Practice

Suppose that you are about to read a story entitled "Lost at Sea," by Gary Paulsen. Answer the following question.

1. What would the title "Lost at Sea" lead you to expect about the events of the story?

Read this passage from "Lost at Sea." Answer the questions below it.

> …For the first time since the storm hit, everything was going well. Then the killer whales found him.
>
> They came silently and with great suddenness at dawn. One second he was sitting alone in the cockpit watching the sun come up over the bowsprit. The next second he heard a massive *woosh!* beside the boat, and a huge black head with distinctive white markings exploded out of the water.
>
> Four other heads rose around the boat, higher and higher until the killer whales towered above him, looking down on him in the cockpit with glistening black eyes, their skins shining in the sun.
>
> He could not move, could not breathe. He had read of them, had talked to Owen of them, and everybody said they didn't harm people. But over him that way looking down on him—they could pluck him up like an appetizer. One snap. They were huge, longer than the boat—living things bigger than his home.

2. What do you think will happen in the next few paragraphs of the story?

____

3. What details in the passage helped you make this prediction?

____

Now read the rest of the passage from "Lost at Sea," and answer the questions below it.

> "My name is Brennan," he said aloud to the whales. "And this is my boat, the *Tadpole*. We mean no harm."
>
> And he meant it, did not feel silly saying it, and with the sound of his voice the whale nearest the boat eased down, blew once and inhaled and was gone. The rest followed. Whether it was his voice or not didn't matter. They were gone and the fear was gone and he was not the same, would never be the same again.
>
> I am, he thought, of the sea—I am of this boat and the sea. I am.

4. How were your predictions about what would happen like the actual events of the story? ____

5. How were your predictions different from the events in the story?

____

____

ACTIVE READING: QUESTION AND CLARIFY

Introduction

Question: Asking yourself questions as you read can help improve your reading comprehension. The first step is identifying what is confusing to you.

Clarify: Often, the answer to your question can be found right in the text, either at an earlier point or later in the text. When you have a question while reading:

- Stop to think.
- Look back over the material you have already read to try to find clues to the answer.
- Continue reading, keeping your question in mind. Often you'll discover the answer later in the text.

Model

Read the passage below from "Paul Bunyan of the North Woods," by Carl Sandburg, and note the interruptor questions in italics.

> Carmack hurried down river to Fortymile to file claims for himself, Jim, and Charlie.
>
> *What does* file claims *mean?*
>
> A claim is a legal right to mine gold, or other minerals, on a specific piece of land.
>
> *Oh, I see. The author explains what a claim is.*
>
> After filing his claims, Carmack proudly walked into a smokey saloon full of miners. In a loud voice, he told the crowd that he had made one of the biggest gold strikes ever. His boast was greeted by a chorus of hoots and disbelief.
>
> *I think making a gold strike must mean finding gold. Maybe I'll learn more about it if I keep reading.*
>
> Why should anyone believe that this man had discovered gold? After all, he was not a "sourdough," someone who has been a prospector for a long time.
>
> *Yes, I was right—a gold strike means discovering gold. A prospector must be someone who goes out looking for gold.*
>
> McCormack backed up his words by pulling out a small bag of gold nuggets. This was all the proof the prospectors needed. The next morning Fortymile was nearly deserted. Its citizens had rushed to stake claims on Rabbit Creek. The great Klondike Gold Rush had begun.

NAME _______________________________   **DATE** ___________

Practice

Below is another passage from "Paul Bunyan of the North Woods," by Carl Sandburg. As you read the passage below, ask yourself questions about what is happening.

Two mosquitoes lighted on one of Paul Bunyan's oxen, killed it, ate it, cleaned the bones, and sat on a grub shanty picking their teeth as Paul came along. Paul sent to Australia for two special bumblebees to kill these mosquitoes. But the bees and the mosquitoes intermarried; their children had stingers on both ends. And things kept getting worse till Paul brought a big boatload of sorghum up from Louisiana and while all the bee-mosquitoes were eating at the sweet sorghum he floated them down to the Gulf of Mexico. They got so fat that it was easy to drown them all between New Orleans and Galveston...

Benny, the Little Blue Ox of Paul Bunyan grew two feet every time Paul looked at him, when a youngster. The barn was gone one morning and they found it on Benny's back; he grew out of it in a night. One night he kept pawing and bellowing for more pancakes, till there were two hundred men at the cook-shanty stove trying to keep him fed. About breakfast time Benny broke loose, tore down the cook-shanty, ate all the pancakes piled up for the loggers' breakfast. And after that Benny made his mistake; he ate the red hot stove; and that finished him. This is only one of the hot-stove stories told in the North Woods.

1. While reading, what questions did you have?

____

____

____

2. What information in the passage helped clarify the answers to these questions?

____

____

____

____

ACTIVE READING: CONNECT

Introduction

There are many ways to respond to something that you are reading. One of the most natural responses is to think about how the literature relates to your own experiences or to another text that you have read. As you read, you may **connect** to a character or something that character says or does. Sometimes, you will be reminded of another story you once read or something that you recently learned. Making connections as you read is important because it allows you to relate to the text in your own personal way.

To make connections to your reading, ask yourself questions such as those below. They will help you to become a more active reader by giving you ideas about how you can connect to what you are reading.

Questions to Help You Connect
- How do I relate to this character?
- Am I like this person? Do I know someone like this person?
- Would I have done or said the same thing as this person?
- Is there anything in this story that is similar to my life, my own experiences, or the experiences of someone that I know?
- In what ways is this story like another story that I have read?

Model

The passage below, from "The Scarlet Ibis," by James Hurst, speaks about a relationship between a boy and his brother who has a disability. As you read it, connect it to your own experiences, ideas, or perhaps another story you have read. The connection you make may be similar to or different from some of the sample connections shown below.

> Although Doodle learned to crawl, he showed no signs of walking, but he wasn't idle. He talked so much that we all quit listening to what he said. It was about this time that Daddy built him a go-cart and I had to pull him around. At first I just paraded him up and down the piazza, but then he started crying to be taken out into the yard and it ended up by my having to lug him wherever I went. If I so much as picked up my cap, he'd start crying to go with me and Mama would call from wherever she was, "Take Doodle with you."

Possible Connections
- I know someone who talks so much that people don't listen to him.
- I have a little brother or sister who always wants to do the things that I do and go everywhere with me.
- Doodle reminds me of my friend's little brother.
- My mother often tells me that I have to take my younger siblings along, and that bothers me.

NAME ______________________________________   **DATE** _______________

Practice

Below is another passage from "The Scarlet Ibis." As you read the
selection, think about how you connect to it and respond by writing
your ideas in the appropriate sections below.

At breakfast on our chosen day, when Mama, Daddy, and Aunt Nicey
were in the dining room, I brought Doodle to the door in the go-cart
just as usual and had them turn their backs, making them cross their
hearts and hope to die if they peeked. I helped Doodle up, and when he
was standing alone I let them look. There wasn't a sound as Doodle
walked slowly across the room and sat down at his place at the table.
Then Mama began to cry and ran over to him, hugging him and kissing
him. Daddy hugged him too, so I went to Aunt Nicey, who was thanks
praying in the doorway, and began to waltz her around. We danced
together quite well until she came down on my big toe with her brogans,
hurting me so badly I thought I was crippled for life.

Doodle told them it was I who had taught him to walk, so everyone
wanted to hug me, and I began to cry.

"What are you crying for?" asked Daddy, but I couldn't answer. They
did not know that I did it for myself: that pride, whose slave I was, spoke
to me louder than all their voices, and that Doodle walked only because
I was ashamed of having a crippled brother.

1. Who do you know that some or all of these characters call to mind?

____

____

2. Which events in this passage remind you of experiences in your own
life? Explain.

____

____

____

3. Do you connect with any of the feelings that the different characters
have? Tell about times that come to your mind when you felt the
same way they did.

____

____

____

4. Does this passage remind you of another story? In what way?

____

____

____

36 Reading Support Practice Book

SQ3R

Introduction

Most of the time, people read for either pleasure or to learn about new things. When "reading to learn," it is helpful to use the **SQ3R** strategy. This strategy helps you understand and remember what you read, especially when you are reading a difficult or unfamiliar text.

SQ3R stands for the five steps a reader can use to remember information.

Survey	Survey the text and get a general idea of what it is about. Try reading the first sentence of each paragraph.
Question	Keep in mind questions you have as you look over the selection. What do you want to find out about in the selection? What looks unclear to you?
Read	Read the text carefully from the beginning. Pause to think about what you are reading and to make sure that you understand it. Look up unknown words and reread difficult sentences or paragraphs.
Recite	See how well you understood and remember the text by reciting what you learned out loud. Recite the information to yourself or to a friend. **Helpful Hint:** Try to answer these questions: Who? What? Where? When? Why? and How?
Review	Summarize the text and think about the main ideas by talking with someone else about it. You may also want to make an outline, use note cards, or make an illustration to help you remember key points.

Practice

Practice using the SQ3R strategy with the passage below. Do not read the entire passage first. Follow the steps below.

I. Survey
What does this passage seem like it will be about?

II. Question
Write some questions that you have.

III. Read
Read the passage. Pause as you read to make sure that you understand it.

Hokusai never stayed long with a period or style, but was always off and running to something new. A great show-off, he painted with his fingers, toothpicks, a bottle, and eggshell; he worked left-handed, from the bottom up, and from left to right. Once he painted two sparrows on a grain of rice. Commissioned by a shogun (a military ruler in 18th century Japan) to decorate a door of the temple of Dempo-ji he tore it off its hinges, laid it in the courtyard, and painted wavy blue lines on it to represent running water, then dipped the feet of a live rooster in red seal ink and chased the bird over the painted door. When the shogun came to see the finished job, he at once saw the river Tatsuta and the falling red maple leaves of autumn. Another time Hokusai used a large broom dipped into a vat of ink to draw the full-length figure of a god, over a hundred feet long, on the floor of a courtyard.

Hokusai did thirty thousand pictures during a full and long life. When he was seventy-five, he wrote:

"From the age of six I had a mania for drawing the shapes of things. When I was fifty I had published a universe of designs. But all I have done before the age of seventy is not worth bothering with. At seventy-five I have learned something of the pattern of nature, of animals, of plants, of trees, birds, fish, and insects. When I am eighty you will see real progress. At ninety I shall have cut my way deeply into the mystery of life itself. At a hundred I shall be a marvelous artist. At a hundred and ten everything I create, a dot, a line, will jump to life as never before. To all of you, I promise to keep my word. I am writing this in my old age. I used to call myself Hokusai, but today I sign myself, "The Old Man Mad About Drawing."

He didn't reach a hundred and ten, but he nearly reached ninety. On the day of his death, in 1849, he was cheerfully at work on a new drawing.

IV. Recite
Verbalize what you have just read by telling yourself or a friend about it.

V. Review
In your notebook, write a brief summary or outline of the passage.

IDENTIFY MAIN IDEAS AND SUPPORTING DETAILS

Introduction

The **main idea** of a passage is its central and most important idea. Effective readers look for this central idea as they read. The main idea can appear at the beginning, middle, or end of a passage.

Writers reinforce their main ideas with **supporting details**. These words, phrases, or sentences tell something about the main idea. They can be facts, statistics, dates, names, opinions, or details.

The main idea of a passage can be stated clearly in one sentence in the selection. This is called a **stated main idea**. Sometimes the main idea is not stated in any one sentence, but is a summary of the information in the passage. This is called an **implied main idea**. When you are reading, begin to identify the main idea, whether stated or implied, and look for its supporting details.

Model 1

In the following example, the underlined sentence is the stated main idea. Each sentence that follows provides support for the idea.

> <u>Travelers to Texas find a variety of vegetation</u>. In the dry regions of West Texas, they see short grasses, cacti, ponderosa pines, and junipers. Mesquite trees and oaks dot the plains of South Texas. Along the coast, travelers enjoy palm trees that blow in the warm breezes. In the Panhandle, they find that grasses cover most of the land.

Model 2

In this example from "A River Comes Home," by Sandra Chisholm Robinson, the main idea is implied rather than stated directly.

> He follows the [Kissimmee] river north. He sees black bears feeding on palmetto berries and deer feeding in the marshes on each side of the river. The green tree tops turn white as thousands of ibis and egrets roost on the branches. Ducks settle in great flocks on the wetlands created by the river. Many fish come to the water's surface to feed on insects. …

The implied main idea might be stated as follows:
Birds, animals, and plants are abundant along the Kissimmee River.

NAME ____   **DATE** ___________

Practice

Part I

Below is a passage from "The Indian All Around Us," by Bernard DeVoto. Read the passage and answer the questions that follow.

> The Europeans who developed into the Americans took over from the Indians many things besides their continent. Look at a few: tobacco, corn, potatoes, beans (kidney, string and lima and therefore succotash), tomatoes, sweet potatoes, squash, popcorn and peanuts, chocolate, pineapples, hominy, Jerusalem artichokes, maple sugar. Moccasins, snowshoes, toboggans, hammocks, ipecac, quinine, the crew haircut, goggles to prevent snow blindness—these are all Indian in origin. So is the versatile boat that helped the white man occupy the continent, the birch-bark canoe, and the custom canoeists have of painting designs on its bow.

1. What statement best expresses the main idea of this passage?

   ____

   ____

   ____

2. Is the main idea implied or stated?

   ____

3. Identify at least ten supporting details in this passage. Write the details in the spaces provided.

   1. ____
   2. ____
   3. ____
   4. ____
   5. ____
   6. ____
   7. ____
   8. ____
   9. ____
   10. ____

NAME ____   **DATE** ___________

Part II
Below is a passage from "A River Comes Home," by Sandra Chisholm Robinson. Read the passage and answer the questions that follow.

> Water that overflowed the river's banks during the rainy season wet the marshes where ducks and other water birds rested and fed. When the wetlands dried up, most of the birds did not return. The deep waters of the canal could not provide for the fish in ways the river had. Soon there were fewer and smaller fish for birds, otters, and people to catch.

1. What statement best expresses the main idea of this passage?

   ____

   ____

   ____

2. Is the main idea implied or stated? _______________________________

   ____

   ____

3. Identify the supporting details in this passage. Write the details in the spaces provided.

   1. ____

   2. ____

   3. ____

Part III

Below is a passage from "Hidden Worlds," by the National Geographic Society. Read the passage and answer the questions that follow.

> A vast cloud of glowing gases called the corona blankets the sun. Reaching hundreds of thousands of miles into space, the corona shines as brightly as a full moon. Yet you cannot normally see the corona. It is hidden in the even greater brilliance of the sun itself.
>
> A total eclipse is a rare event that lasts only a few minutes. But astronomers all over the world wait for that short period when the moon masks the sun. The sun's energy is constantly being filtered through the gases of corona. Scientists study the corona to learn more about that energy and its effects on earth.
>
> The next total eclipse of the sun visible from North America will not occur until the year 2017. Several partial eclipses will occur before then. During a partial eclipse, only part of the sun's surface is hidden. The corona remains invisible.

1. What statement best expresses the main idea of this passage?

   ____

   ____

   ____

2. Is the main idea implied or stated? ______________________________

3. Identify the supporting details in this passage. Write the details in the spaces provided.

   1. ____

   2. ____

   3. ____

MAKE INFERENCES

Introduction

Writers don't always describe everything that is happening. It is up to the reader to figure out why characters may be acting or feeling a certain way. When readers draw these types of conclusions they are **making inferences**. Often, making inferences requires readers to "read between the lines." Your own experiences and prior knowledge about people, places, ideas, and events will help you to make inferences or reasonable guesses as you read. In addition, use whatever textual clues there are in order to draw certain conclusions. These inferences will help you to better understand the selection and what the author is trying to communicate.

Keep this equation in mind to understand how you make inferences.

Textual Clues   +   What You Know   =   Inference

Model

Read the passage below from "Chee's Daughter," by Juanita Platero and Siyowin Miller. Then look at the chart to see how certain inferences were made.

> Wind warmed by the sun touched his high-boned cheeks like flicker feathers, and still he rode on silently, deeper into Little Canyon, until the red rock walls rose straight upward from the stream bed and only a narrow piece of blue sky hung above.
>
> This was his home—this wide place in the canyon—levels of jagged rock and levels of rich red earth. This was home to Chee, the rider of the buckskin, as it had been to many generations before him.

Textual Clues	+	What You Know	=	Inference
The wind felt like flicker feathers		this probably hurt		Chee is not a complainer
Chee is described as the rider of the buckskin and his ancestors have been in this land for generations		Chee sounds like an American Indian name and Indians inhabited regions for generations		Chee is probably a Native American

NAME ____ **DATE** ______________

Practice

Below is another passage from "Chee's Daughter." As you read it, look for clues that help you make inferences about what is happening. Then answer the questions that follow.

> Then the smile faded from Chee's lips and his eyes darkened as he tied his horse to a corral post and turned to the strangely empty compound. "Someone has told them," he thought, "and they are inside weeping." He passed his mother's deserted loom on the south side of the hogan and pulled the rude wooden door toward him, bowing his head, hunching his shoulders to get inside.
>
> His mother sat sideways by the center fire, her feet drawn up under her full skirts. Her hands were busy kneading dough in the chipped white basin. With her head down, her voice was muffled when she said, "The meal will soon be ready, son."
>
> Chee passed his father sitting against the wall, hat over his eyes as though asleep. He passed his older sister who sat turning mutton ribs on a crude wire grill over the coals, noticed tears dropping on her hands. "She cared more for my wife than I realized," he thought.
>
> Then because something had to be said sometime, he tossed the black Stetson upon a bulging sack of wool and said, "You have heard then." He could not shut from his mind how confidently he had set the handsome new hat on his head that very morning, slanting the wide brim over one eye: he was going to see his wife and today he would ask the doctors about bringing her home; last week she had looked so much better.

1. What inference can you make about how everyone is feeling?

   ____

   What clues helped you make this inference?

   ____

2. What inference can you make about the relationship between Chee's sister and Chee's wife?

   ____

   What clues helped you make this inference?

   ____

3. What inference can you make about what happened to Chee's wife?

   ____

   ____

4. What clues helped you make this inference?

   ____

   ____

CLASSIFY/CATEGORIZE

Introduction

When you **classify** or **categorize**, you arrange things into classes or groups according to a system. For example, dogs and cats are both classified as animals, but each can be further classified into different types of dogs or cats.

   This chart may help clarify the relationship of the things to be classified and their division into groups.

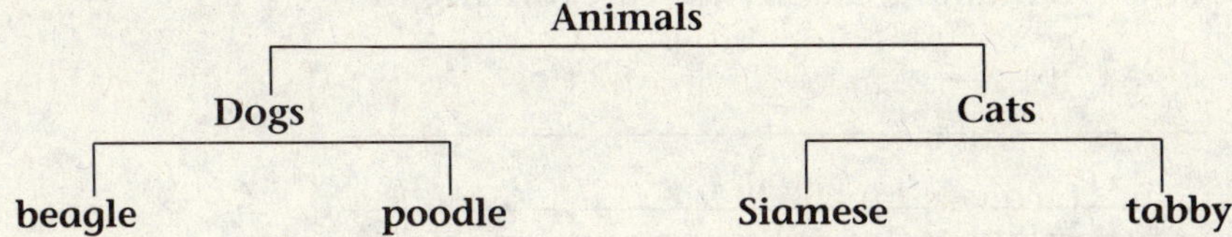

   In much of your reading, you will come upon examples of classification. Classifying is a technique that writers use to organize a passage. Writers help readers understand a point they are making by classifying ideas or things into a group. While you are reading, look for examples of this technique. Notice how classifying helps you recognize similarities and differences in a subject and helps explain an idea by providing specific examples or details.

Model

Look at the following passage from "Abe Lincoln Grows Up," by Carl Sandburg.

> …[Lincoln] got hold of "Aesop's Fables," "Pilgrim's Progress," "Robinson Crusoe", and Weems's "The Life of Francis Marion." The book of fables, written or collected thousands of years ago by the Greek slave, known as Aesop, sank deep in his mind. As he read through the book a second and third time, he had a feeling there were fables all around him, that everything he saw and learned had a fable wrapped in it somewhere.

Above, Carl Sandburg classifies/categorizes the literature Lincoln possessed: *Aesop's Fables, Pilgrim's Progress, Robinson Crusoe,* and *The Life of Francis Marion.* These pieces of literature could further be classified into groups according to their impact on Lincoln.

Minor Impact on Lincoln	Major Impact on Lincoln
Pilgrim's Progress *Robinson Crusoe* *The Life of Francis Marion*	*Aesop's Fables*

Practice

Below is another passage from "Abe Lincoln Grows Up," by Carl Sandburg. Read the passage and follow the instructions below.

The farm boys in their evenings at Jones's store in Gentryville talked about how Abe Lincoln was always reading, digging into books, stretching out flat on his stomach in front of the fireplace, studying till midnight, picking a piece of charcoal to write on the fire shovel, shaving off what he wrote, and then writing more—till midnight and past midnight.

1. What kinds of things or ideas is Sandburg classifying/categorizing in this passage?

   ____

   ____

2. What does the classifying of these examples tell you about Lincoln's view of reading and writing?

   ____

   ____

3. How does the classifying of his reading and writing activities aid your understanding of what Abe Lincoln was like as a boy?

   ____

   ____

4. **Challenge!**
   Choose an interest of yours that is a high priority in your life. It might be a sport you play, a hobby, studying, reading, watching television, or spending time with your friends. As Sandburg classified Lincoln's reading activities, write a paragraph that classifies your activities to show how important this special interest is to you.

   ____

   ____

   ____

   ____

   ____

   ____

   ____

   ____

COMPARE AND CONTRAST

Introduction

As you read, look for the writer's use of comparisons and contrasts. A writer uses **comparison** to show how things are similar and uses **contrast** to show how things are different. While reading, look for clue words that may help you recognize a comparison or contrast. Clue words that may signal a comparison are *like, similar to,* and *in the same way.* Clue words that may signal a contrast are *but, different from,* and *however.*

Model

In "Letter from a Concentration Camp," by Yoshiko Uchida, Jimbo is trying to explain to his pal Hermie what it's like being in the Assembly Center. Look for the comparisons and contrasts and compare them to the ones below.

> You know what? It's like being in jail here—not being free to live in your own house, do what you want, or eat what you want. They've got barbed wire all around this racetrack and guard towers at each corner to make sure we can't get out. Doesn't that sound like a prison? It sure feels like one!

Comparison
- There's barbed wire all around the area.
- There are guard towers at each corner.

These statements show how being in the Assembly Center is similar to being in jail (something familiar).

Contrast
- You can't do what you want.
- You can't eat what you want.

These statements show how being in the Assembly Center is different from being in your own house.

Practice

Below is another passage from "Letter from a Concentration Camp," by Yoshiko Uchida. Read the passage and answer the question below.

> Well, Hermie, I gotta go now. Mama says we should get to the showers before the hot water runs out like it did when she went to do the laundry. Tomorrow she's getting up at 4:00 A.M. to beat the crowd. Can you imagine having to get up in the middle of the night and stand in line to wash your sheets and towels? By hand too! No luxuries like washing machines in this dump!

1. How does washing clothes in the Assembly Center contrast with washing clothes at home?

   ____

   ____

2. Circle the clue words that help you recognize comparisons and contrasts.
   a. It's like being in jail here.
   b. During World War II Japanese Americans were treated differently than German Americans.
   c. Jimbo and Hermie are pals even though Jimbo is Japanese and Hermie is German.
   d. Both Jimbo and Hermie love dogs.
   e. You don't have to mow the lawn at the Assembly Center; however, it's not a resort.
   f. Hermie gets to eat what he wants while Jimbo must eat cold potatoes.
   g. Jimbo feels that the Assembly Center is similar to a concentration camp.
   h. I washed my clothes in the same way my grandmother did— by hand.
   i. In contrast to being at home, being in an Assembly Center is hard.
   j. Although we usually see eye to eye, today we disagree.

3. **Challenge!**
   Research living conditions in another country. List five comparisons and five contrasts to living in your country.

	Compare	Contrast
1.		
2.		
3.		
4.		
5.		

FOLLOW A SEQUENCE OF EVENTS

The **sequence of events** in a passage is the chronological, or time, order of those events.

While you read, in order to help you follow the sequence of events, you may want to make a timeline. A timeline not only enables you to follow the series of events but to see the pattern of events that is developing. To make a timeline, draw a horizontal line. Draw a short vertical line for each important event in the sequence. At each vertical line, write a few words describing the event.

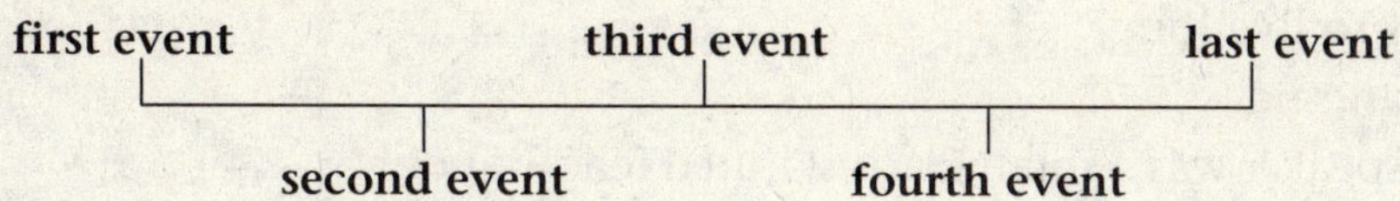

Helpful Hint: Look for clue words that may signal a sequence, such as *first*, *second*, *next*, *then*, *finally*, and *last*.

Model

Make a timeline from this passage from "Hammerman," by Adrien Stoutenburg, and compare it to the one below.

> The story seems to be that when John Henry was a baby, the first thing he reached for was a hammer, which was hung nearby on the cabin wall.
>
> John Henry's father put his arm around his wife's shoulder. "He's going to grow up to be a steel-driving man. I can see it plain as rows of cotton running uphill."
>
> As John Henry grew a bit older, he practiced swinging the hammer, not hitting at things, but just enjoying the feel of it whooshing against the air. When he was old enough to talk, he told everyone, "I was born with a hammer in my hand."
>
> John Henry was still a boy when the Civil War started, but he was a big, hard-muscled boy, and he could outwork and outplay all the other boys on the plantation.
>
> "You're going to be a mighty man, John Henry," his father told him.

Timeline

1. John Henry reaches for a hammer (infant)

2. Father says, "He's going to grow up to be a steel-driving man."

3. John Henry practices swinging hammer (a bit older)

4. John Henry tells everyone he was born with a hammer in his hand.

5. John Henry outworks and outplays the other boys on the plantation.

Practice

1. Timeline

Make a timeline from this passage from "Hammerman," by Adrien Stoutenburg. The horizontal line has already been drawn for you.

John Henry didn't move. He got a stubborn look around his jaw. "You loan me a hammer, mister, and if somebody will hold the spike for me, I'll prove what I can do."

The three men who had just finished driving in a spike looked toward him and laughed. One of them said, "Anybody who would hold a spike for a greenhorn don't want to live long."

"I'll hold it," a fourth man said.

John Henry saw that the speaker was a small, dark-skinned fellow about his own age.

The foreman asked the small man, "D'you aim to get yourself killed, Li'l Willie?"

Li'l Willie didn't answer. He knelt and set a spike down through the rail on the crosstie. "Come on, big boy," he said.

John Henry picked up one of the sheepnose hammers lying in the cinders. He hefted it and decided it was too light. He picked up a larger one which weighed twelve pounds. The handle was lead and limber and greased with tallow to make it smooth.

Everyone was quiet, watching, as he stepped over to the spike.

John Henry swung the hammer over his shoulder so that the hammer head hung down against the back of his knees. He felt a thrill run through his arms and chest.

"Tap it down gentle, first," said Li'l Willie.

But John Henry had already started to swing. He brought the hammer flashing down, banging the spike squarely on the head. Before the other men could draw a breath of surprise, the hammer flashed again, whirring through the air like a giant hummingbird. One more swing, and the spike was down, its steel head smoking from the force of the blow.

The foreman blinked, swallowed, and blinked again. "Man," he told John Henry, "you're hired!"

2. Questions

Use your timeline to answer the following questions.
- What is the first event?
- What does John Henry do?
- What is the conclusion?

USE VISUAL AND GRAPHIC CLUES

Introduction

When you read, you can learn all kinds of information. Some information, however, does not come from words. **Visual and graphic aids** are pictorial representations that also help you learn about a subject. Visual and graphic sources of information include the following:

diagrams	lists	maps	charts
illustrations	scale drawings	schedules	diagrams
tables	timelines	graphs	cartoons

One kind of visual or graphic aid that you may encounter in social studies textbooks or magazine articles is a map. Political maps are flat pictures that show places on the earth, including different countries or states, major cities, rivers, highways, and so on. Political maps may include the following features:

- a *compass rose* that shows where north, south, east, and west are located
- a *map scale* that shows the relationship between actual distances and map distances

Study this map. Find the compass rose and map scale.

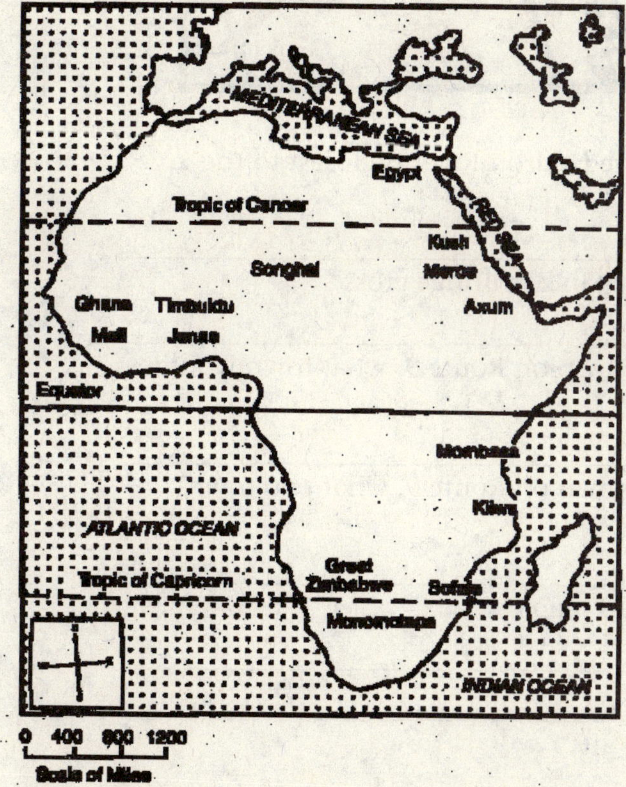

Practice

Washington Irving set such stories as "Rip Van Winkle" and "The Legend of Sleepy Hollow" in the Hudson River Valley where he lived. The map below shows what part of this area looks like today. Use the map to answer the questions that follow.

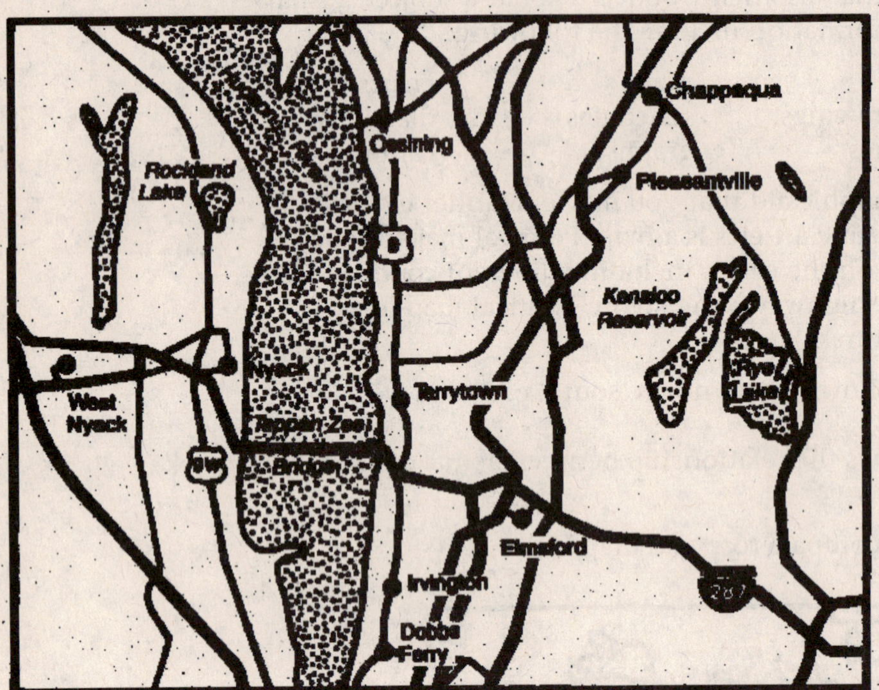

1. What town on the east side of the Hudson River is closest to the Tappan Zee Bridge?

   ____

2. What body of water does the Tappan Zee Bridge cross?

   ____

3. If you traveled north from Tarrytown on Route 9, what town would you reach?

   ____

4. If you traveled south from Tarrytown on Route 9, what two towns would you reach?

   ____

5. What two lakes are shown on this map?

   ____

   ____

ADJUST READING RATE

Introduction

Every day you read a variety of different materials, from TV guides to newspaper headlines to the instructions on a math test. You read some materials more quickly than others. The speed at which you read is called your **reading rate**. You adjust your reading rate depending on what you are reading and what your purpose is for reading. For example, when you read a story for entertainment, you probably read fairly quickly. On the other hand, when you read a textbook or a magazine article to learn important information, you read more slowly and carefully.

Which of the following—a fairy tale, a chapter about space travel, or a letter from a friend—do you think you would read most quickly? Most slowly? Choosing an appropriate reading rate will help you get the most out of what you read. Before you begin to read, follow these steps to determine which reading rate is right for you:

1. First, consider your purpose for reading.
2. Then, look at the selection to find out how difficult it is to read.
3. Finally, decide whether you should read the selection at a faster, average, or slower rate.

The following guidelines may help you adjust your reading rate to suit your purpose and the type of material that you are going to read:

- When you read to learn information or when you read difficult selections that contain unfamiliar words and ideas, read slowly and carefully.
- Read more quickly when you read for entertainment or when you read fairly easy selections about subjects with which you are familiar.

Reading Tips

- Two strategies that will help you read more quickly and efficiently are skimming and scanning. **Skim** a selection to get a general impression about the topic. Do not read every word but look at the selection quickly, noticing the title, headings, words in boldface or italic type, and visual and graphic clues. Skimming a selection before you read will help you determine which reading rate to use.
- **Scan** a selection to find specific information, such as dates and important facts. Read quickly, moving your eyes over the page to locate key words that will help you find the information that you want.
- When you want to learn information and remember details, do a **close reading**. Read the entire selection slowly word for word.

Practice

Below is a passage about the African American folk hero John Henry.
Before you read, skim the passage to determine which reading rate you
will use. Consider why you are reading this passage and how difficult it is
for you to read. Then read the passage, using the reading rate that you
selected, and answer the questions that follow the poem.

> John Henry started on the right hand,
> The steam drill started on the lef'—
> 'Before I'd let this steam drill beat me down,
> I'd hammer my fool self to death,
> Lawd, Lawd, I'd hammer my fool self to death.'
>
> John Henry had a lil woman,
> Her name were Polly Ann,
> John Henry took sick an' had to go to bed,
> Polly Ann drove steel like a man.
>
> Lawd, Lawd, Polly Ann drove steel like a man.
> John Henry said to his shaker,[1]
> 'Shaker, why don' you sing?
> I'm throwin' twelve poun's from my hips on down,
> Jes' listen to the col' steel ring,
> Lawd, Lawd, jes' listen to the col' steel ring.'
>
> Oh, the captain said to John Henry,
> 'I b'lieve this mountain's sinkin' in.'
> John Henry said to his captain, oh my!
> 'Ain' nothing' but my hammer suckin' win',
> Lawd, Lawd, ain' nothin' but my hammer suckin' win'.'

1. **shaker** (shā' kər), *n.*: Person who sets the spikes and places the drills for a steel-driver to
hammer.

1. What reading rate—faster, average, or slower—did you select for
reading this passage?

____

2. Why did you choose this reading rate?

____

3. **Challenge!**
Find three different types of selections that you are likely to read. (For
example, you might consider a magazine article, a comic book, a science
textbook, a recipe, a short story, or another type of selection.) Skim each
selection you choose, and decide at what rate you would read it—a faster
rate, an average rate, or a slower rate. On a separate sheet of paper,
explain why you chose the rate you did for each selection.

NAME _________________________________   DATE __________

ACTIVE READING: ACTIVATE PRIOR KNOWLEDGE

Introduction

What you know before you open a book may decide how you will react
to it. Using the knowledge you already have about a particular subject
can make what you read easier to understand.

In most cases, the subject of an article or story will become clear to you
once you have read the first paragraph or two of a piece of writing. At
that point, you may want to stop and ask yourself what you already
know about the subject.

Reading Tip

Activate prior knowledge by asking yourself the following questions:
1. What is the subject of this piece of writing?
2. What do I already know about this subject?
3. Have I ever read about this subject before? If so, what specific details
   did I learn about it?

Model

Below are the first two paragraphs of an article called "All Names Are
American Names," by Kie Ho. Identify the subject of the paragraphs.
Then quickly list a few things you know about it on a sheet of paper.
Compare your answers to the model below.

> At a recent seminar that my company sponsored, where many of the par-
> ticipants came from our overseas offices, a gentleman from the Netherlands
> looked at my name tag and said, "I see that you are from our division in
> California, but your name does not sound American." I told him that
> mine is indeed a Chinese name; however, I am an American citizen.
>
> I should have told him that my name is as American as Lucille LeSueur
> or Margarita Carman Cansino before they became Joan Crawford and
> Rita Hayworth. My name does sound as foreign as the name of the
> Japanese slugger Sadaharu Oh, but does it not also sound as American as
> Joe DiMaggio?

Subject: What makes a name an American name?
1. What I already know:
   • Many people brought names to this country from other
     countries.
   • A name alone doesn't determine whether or not somebody is
     American.
   • Sometimes you can tell from a name where a person's ancestors
     lived.
2. What I've read about this subject before:
   • I read a book about Hollywood stars that told what their
     original names had been and why they changed them.

Practice

Below is another passage from "All Names Are American Names," by Kie Ho. Answer the questions that follow it.

When our daughter was born, we did not give her a Chinese name. We thought that the name should be selected for the child, not for the parents' sake. We would have liked to name her May Hoa Ho, "Ho the Pretty Flower," but imagine the problems that she would face in school among children who like to make fun of "funny" names. So we gave her a "common" American name: Melanie. We hope that she will be as gentle as Melanie Wilkes in "Gone with the Wind." I wonder if Melanie Wilkes' mother ever knew that "Melanie" refers to something black: Would she still have named her so? Only Margaret Mitchell could tell.

So what's in a name? Benjamin Kubelsky changed his name (Jack Benny). Zbigniew Brzezinski[1] did not. I will not, either.

____

1. Zbigniew Brzezinski (zuh BEEG nyev breh ZHEEN skee): National security advisor to President Carter, 1977–1981.

1. How did you get your first and last names? Are you named after anyone? Has your family name been the same over many generations? Explain below.

   ____

   ____

2. Do you know anything about the methods used to name people in other cultures? If you do, explain them below.

   ____

   ____

3. From your experience, do children with unusual names have a hard time in school? Can you think of an incident illustrating this? If so, describe it below.

   ____

   ____

4. Do you know about any famous people who have changed their names? List them below and, if possible, give the old name and the new name.

   ____

   ____

   ____

KWL

Introduction

KWL is a strategy that you can use to organize your thoughts before and after you read a selection. KWL stands for what you **know**, what you **want** to know, and what you **learn**. Although organizing your ideas in this fashion may seem very basic, KWL is a truly helpful way to think about and remember information. It gets you thinking about a topic before you read about it, and it encourages you to ask questions that interest you and to try to find answers to these questions through your reading. A chart like the one below will help you to use the KWL strategy. Simply follow these three steps:

Model

Step 1	Step 2	Step 3
K What You **Know**	**W** What You **Want to Know**	**L** What You **Learn**

The passage below is from "Two Kinds," by Amy Tan. By knowing the topic of the selection or by reading the first sentence or two of it, you can complete the first two steps in the KWL strategy. Then, as you read the passage, you can jot down what you Learn. Read the passage and then look at the sample KWL chart to see how one reader used the technique to help read the passage.

> My mother believed you could be anything you wanted to be in America. You could open a restaurant. You could work for the government and get a good retirement. You could buy a house with almost no money down. You could become rich. You could become instantly famous. America was where all my mother's hopes lay. She had come here in 1949 after losing everything in China: her mother and father, her family home, her first husband, and two daughters, twin baby girls.

K What you **Know**	**W** What you **Want to Know**	**L** What you **Learn**
• Parents often tell their children that they can be anything they want to be.	• I want to know what this mother will hope for her daughter	• Amy Tan's mother had a difficult life and dreams of a better life for her child.
• Many immigrants hope that America will be the land of opportunity	• I want to know what Amy Tan became.	

NAME _______________________________   **DATE** _____________

Practice

The passage below is also from "Two Kinds," by Amy Tan. It is about how Amy Tan's mother used to test her every night while they ate dinner. From that information, write down **what you know** and **what you want to know**. Then read the passage and complete the section in the chart for **what you learn.**

Every night at dinner, my mother and I would sit at the Formica kitchen table. She would present new tests, taking her examples from stories of amazing children she had read in *Ripley's Believe It or Not,* or *Good Housekeeping, Reader's Digest,* and a dozen other magazines she kept in a pile in our bathroom. My mother got these magazines from people whose houses she cleaned. And since she cleaned many houses each week, we had a great assortment. She would look through them all, searching for stories about remarkable children.

The first night she brought out a story about a three-year-old boy who knew the capitals of all the states and even most of the European countries. A teacher was quoted as saying the little boy could also pronounce the names of the foreign cities correctly. "What's the capital of Finland?" my mother asked me, looking at the magazine story.

The tests got harder—multiplying numbers in my head, finding the queen of hearts in a deck of cards, trying to stand on my head without using my hands, predicting the daily temperatures in Los Angeles, New York, and London. One night I had to look at a page from the Bible for three minutes and then report everything I could remember.

K What you **Know**	W What you **Want to Know**	L What you **Learn**

NAME ________________________   DATE ________

DISTINGUISH BETWEEN IMPORTANT AND UNIMPORTANT INFORMATION

Introduction

Writers use a variety of details to discuss a topic or tell a story. The details may be supporting details that back up main ideas or descriptive details that help create images of persons, places, things, events, or experiences. Some details may be more important than others. By learning to distinguish between important and unimportant information, readers can focus on what is worth remembering.

Important information can appear throughout a piece of literature, not just in the opening and closing paragraphs or passages. Study the following steps that a reader can take to distinguish between important and unimportant information:

5. Explain why this information is important or unimportant.
4. Ask yourself, "Should I remember this information?"
3. Identify the details the writer gives.
2. Decide what it is about.
1. Read the whole passage.

Model

Use the steps to help you identify the important and less important information in this passage from "The Gymnast," by Gary Soto. Compare your answers to the ones below.

> For three days of my eleventh summer I listened to my mother yap about my cousin, Issac, who was taking gymnastics. She was proud of him, she said one evening at the stove as she pounded a round steak into *carne asada* and crushed a heap of beans into refritos. I was jealous because I had watched my share of "Wide World of Sports" and knew that people admired an athlete who could somersault without hurting himself. I pushed aside my solitary game of Chinese checkers and spent a few minutes rolling around the backyard until I was dizzy and itchy with grass.

Important Information
- Narrator's mother admired his cousin who was taking gymnastics.
- Narrator was jealous of his cousin.

These ideas are important because they reveal the conflict the narrator was experiencing.

Less Important Information
- Details about food: his mother was preparing *carne asada* and *refritos*.

These details do not help the reader understand the feelings of the narrator.

Practice

Part I

Here is another passage from "The Gymnast," by Gary Soto. Read the passage and then fill in the chart.

I ate the plums and watched him until he was sweaty and out of breath. When he was finished, I begged him to let me wear his cloth shoes. Drops of sweat fell at his feet. He looked at me with disdain, ran a yellow towel across his face, and patted his neck dry. He tore the white tape from his wrists—I liked the tape as well and tried to paste it around my wrists. He washed off his hands. I asked him about the white powder, and he said it kept his hands dry. I asked him why he needed dry hands to do cartwheels and backflips. He said that all gymnasts kept their hands dry, then drank from a bottle of greenish water he said was filled with nutrients.

What is the passage about?		
What details are given?	**Should I remember this information?**	**Why or why not?**

NAME _______________________________   **DATE** ___________

Part II

Read the following article about the panda written by E. Lendell Cockrum for *The World Book Encyclopedia.* If you were preparing a report comparing the physical characteristics of the two kinds of pandas, which information from this article would you include? Which information would you not include?

At the bottom of this page, note the information that would be less important to your report. Explain why you would not include it. Then fill in the map on the next page.

Panda is one of two kinds of rare animals that live in mountainous areas of Tibet and southern China. The two kinds are not related. Both kinds feed mainly on bamboo shoots.

The *giant panda* has a white, chubby body with black legs and shoulders. Its face is white with a round, black spot at each eye. The giant panda is difficult to find. Scientists in Europe considered them a myth until the middle 1800's. A live giant panda was first brought to the United States in 1936.

The *lesser panda*, sometimes called the *Himalayan raccoon*, is about the size of a cat. Its body is more or less raccoon-shaped, and is reddish-brown with white face markings. Its long tail has alternating reddish-brown and yellow rings.

Scientific Classification. Giant pandas belong to the bear family, *Ursidae.* They are genus *Ailuropoda,* species *A. melanoleuca.* Lesser pandas belong to the raccoon family, *Procyonidae,* and are genus *Ailurus,* species *A. fulgens.*

Less important information:

1. ____

2. ____

3. ____

4. ____

Why?

1. ____

2. ____

3. ____

4. ____

NAME _______________________________   **DATE** _______________

Part III

Fill in the center circle with your topic and the outer circles with
subtopics. Write important details on the lines. Explain your selections.

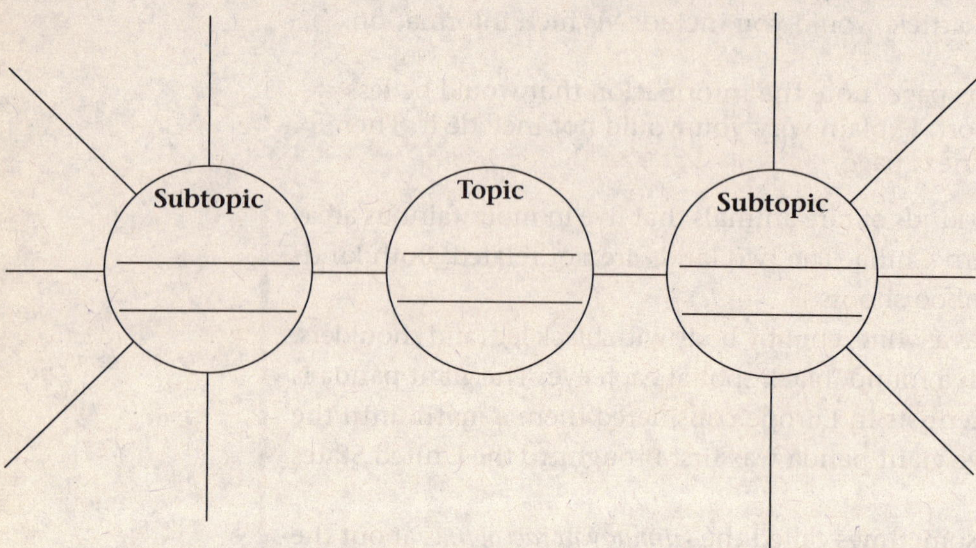

Why I chose these details:

____

____

____

____

NAME ____   DATE ____________

DISTINGUISH BETWEEN FACT AND OPINION OR NONFACT

Introduction

A text may contain facts, nonfacts, and opinions. In order to evaluate
what they are reading, readers need to be aware of the distinction
between fact and opinion or fact and nonfact. A **fact** is a statement that
can be proved to be true. Ways to prove facts include using reference
sources, observation, and prior knowledge. An **opinion** is the writer's
personal feeling or belief. An opinion may not be false, but it cannot be
proved to be true. A **nonfact** is a statement based on guessing. It
contains no evidence for proof.

Helpful Hints

Readers can look for certain words or phrases that signal opinions.
Examples of these signal words and phrases include the following:

I think	*pretty*	*good*	*bad*
I believe	*attractive*	*wonderful*	*terrible*
probably	*ugly*	*safe*	*dangerous*

Model

The following paragraph from "The All-American Slurp," by Lensey
Namioka, contains statements that express facts and opinions. Notice the
underlined signal words.

> Mrs. Gleason offered the relish tray to Mother. The tray looked <u>pretty</u>, with
> its tiny red radishes, curly sticks of carrots, and long, slender stalks of pale
> green celery. "Do try some of the celery, Mrs. Lin," she said. "It's from a
> local farmer, and it's <u>sweet</u>."

Facts	Opinion
The radishes are red.	The tray looked pretty
The carrot sticks are curly.	The celery is sweet.
The celery stalks are pale green.	
The celery is from a local farmer.	

These statements can be proved to be true

These statements express the opinions of the narrator and the character Mrs. Gleason.

Now read the statement below. Decide if this statement is fact, nonfact,
or opinion.

> If you ask me, sliced, curled vegetables are less nutritious than vegetables
> that are left whole.

You're right if you decided that the statement is nonfact. This statement
is based on pure guesswork. There is no evidence to support it, and it may
be proved to be untrue.

NAME _______________________________   **DATE** ___________

Practice

Part I

Below is another passage from "The All-American Slurp," by Lensey Namioka. Read the passage and decide which statements are facts and which are opinions. Fill in the chart.

> Mother decided not to take a chance with chicken gizzards. Since we had western guests, she set the table with large dinner plates, which we never used in Chinese meals. In fact we didn't use individual plates at all, but picked up food from the platters in the middle of the table and brought it directly to our rice bowls. Following the practice of Chinese-American restaurants, Mother also placed large serving spoons on the platters.
>
> The dinner started well. Mrs. Gleason exclaimed at the beautifully arranged dishes of food: the colorful candied fruit in the sweet-and-sour pork dish, the noodle-thin shreds of chicken meat stir-fried with tiny peas, and the glistening pink prawns in a ginger sauce.

Statement or Idea	Fact?	Opinion?	Why?

NAME ______________________________   **DATE** __________

Part II

The following passage is taken from "The America Idea," by Theodore
H. White. Read the passage and look for facts and nonfacts. Answer
the questions.

> The idea was there at the very beginning, well before Thomas Jefferson
> put it into words—and the idea rang the call.
>
> Jefferson himself could not have imagined the reach of his call across
> the world in time to come when he wrote:
>
> "We hold these truths to be self-evident, that all men are created equal,
> that they are endowed by their Creator with certain unalienable rights,
> that among these are life, liberty, and the pursuit of happiness."
>
> But over the next two centuries the call would reach the potato patches
> of Ireland, the ghettoes of Europe, the paddyfields of China, stirring
> farmers to leave their lands and townsmen their trades and thus unset-
> tling all traditions.
>
> It is the call from Thomas Jefferson, embodied in the great statue that
> looks down the Narrows of New York Harbor, and in the immigrants who
> answered the call, that we now celebrate.

1. What facts can you find in this passage? How can they be proved?

____

____

____

____

____

____

2. What nonfacts can you find in this passage? How do you know?

____

____

____

____

____

____

     Distinguish Between Fact and Opinion or Nonfact   **65**

NAME ____ **DATE** _____________

Part III

Here is another passage from "The American Idea," by Theodore H. White. Read it carefully and identify at least one fact, one opinion, and one nonfact. Give reasons for your decisions.

The new Americans were tough men fighting for a very tough idea. How they won their battles is a story for the schoolbooks, studied by scholars, wrapped in myths by historians and poets. But what is most important is the story of the idea that made them into a nation, the idea that had an explosive power undreamed of in 1776.

All other nations had come into being among people whose families had lived for time out of mind on the same land where they were born. Englishmen are English, Frenchmen are French, Chinese are Chinese, while their governments come and go; their national states can be torn apart and remade without losing their nationhood. But Americans are a nation born of an idea; not the place, but the idea, created the United States Government.

The story we celebrate is the story of how this idea worked itself out, how it stretched and changed and how the call for "life, liberty and the pursuit of happiness" does still, as it did in the beginning, mean different things to different people.

Fact: **Reason:**

_______________________ _______________________

_______________________ _______________________

_______________________ _______________________

Opinion: **Reason:**

_______________________ _______________________

_______________________ _______________________

_______________________ _______________________

Nonfact: **Reason:**

_______________________ _______________________

_______________________ _______________________

_______________________ _______________________

NAME ________________________________ DATE ________

EVALUATE AUTHOR'S PURPOSE AND POINT OF VIEW

Introduction

What different kinds of written materials: newspaper articles, travel brochures, recipes, magazine ads, instruction manuals, stories, postcards, speeches, textbook chapters, or poems—have you read this week? For what purpose was each of these pieces written? An **author's purpose** is the main reason that he or she has for writing.

An author's purpose may be one of the following:

- To entertain
- To persuade
- To describe
- To inform

For example, an author's main reason for writing a play or a story may be to entertain. A travel brochure about a tropical island is written to describe, and a letter to the editor is written to persuade. An author's purpose in writing an encyclopedia article is to inform. Being able to recognize why an author wrote a particular piece will help you to determine how you will read it and to better appreciate what you read.

The perspective an author takes when writing is called **point of view.** When you read nonfiction, or factual writing about real people, places, and events, the author's point of view is his or her opinions or attitudes toward a subject. By reading a selection carefully and by noting details, you can draw conclusions about an author's ideas and feelings.

When you read fiction, or writing about imaginary people, places, and events, the story is told from the point of view of an imaginary character. An author may tell a story from first-person or third-person point of view. The chart below shows the differences between these points of view.

First Person	Third Person
A character in the story tells what happens, using the pronouns *I, me,* and *we.*	A narrator who is not one of the characters in the story tells what happens, using the pronouns *he, she,* and *it.*

NAME _________________________________ **DATE** ___________

Practice

A. Read the passage below from "Eleven", a story by Sandra Cisneros.
   Then complete the sentences that follow.

> What they don't understand about birthdays and what they never tell
> you is that when you're eleven, you're also ten, and nine, and eight, and
> seven, and six, and five, and four, and three, and two, and one. And
> when you wake up on your eleventh birthday you expect to feel eleven,
> but you don't. You open your eyes and everything's just like yesterday,
> only it's today. And you don't feel eleven at all. You feel like you're still
> ten. And you are—underneath the year that makes you eleven.
>
> Like some days you might say something stupid, and that's the part of
> you that's still ten. Or maybe some days you might need to sit on your
> mama's lap because you're scared, and that's the part of you that's five.
> And maybe one day when you're all grown up maybe you will need to
> cry like if you're three, and that's okay. That's what I tell Mama when she's
> sad and needs to cry. Maybe she's feeling three.

1. The author's purpose is _______________________________________

   ____

   ____

2. The point of view is ____

   ____

   ____

B. **Challenge!**
   Complete the chart below. List three different works of fiction or
   nonfiction that you have recently read. Then identify the author's
   purpose and point of view.

What I Have Read	Author's Purpose	Point of View

NAME ____   **DATE** ___________

DRAW CONCLUSIONS

Introduction

Alert readers know how to use the facts and evidence in a text to draw
conclusions. **Drawing conclusions** means making judgments about
what has happened or what you have learned in your reading. The type
of conclusions a reader can draw depends upon the kind of writing. For
instance, if you were reading a mystery story, putting together the supporting facts would help you draw a conclusion about who the murderer
was or how the murder was committed. If you were reading a persuasive
essay, supporting facts might help you come to a conclusion about the
author's opinion. Writers usually lead the reader to a conclusion by
arranging their facts in an orderly way. When you read, use a diagram
like the following to keep track of the facts and the conclusions you can
draw from them:

Supporting Facts
Conclusion

Model

What conclusions can you draw from the supporting facts in this passage
from "Cat on the Go," a true story from the life of veterinarian James
Herriot. Compare your answers to the ones below.

> The door opened and Helen came in. "You've been a long time, Jim."
> She walked over to the table and looked down at the sleeping cat. "What
> a poor skinny little thing. He's all bones."
>
> "You should have seen him when he came in." Tristan switched off
> the sterilizer and screwed shut the valve on the anesthetic machine. "He
> looks a lot better now."
>
> She stroked the little animal for a moment. "Is he badly injured?"
>
> "I'm afraid so, Helen," I said. "We've done our best for him but I
> honestly don't think he has much chance."

1. Supporting Facts: Helen feels the operation has taken an awfully long
   time. Helen notices how skinny the cat is.
   Conclusion: Helen is worried about the cat.
2. Supporting Facts: The narrator says the cat is badly injured. The
   narrator admits that the cat doesn't have much of a chance for survival.
   Conclusion: The cat is in danger of dying.

Practice

Part I

This passage is followed by three conclusions. List the supporting facts above the conclusions that are correct and cross out the conclusions that are wrong.

"What's happened?" I asked.

"It's Oscar—he's gone!"

"Gone? What do you mean?"

"Oh Jim, I think he's run away."

I stared at her. "He wouldn't do that. He often goes down to the garden at night. Are you sure he isn't there?"

"Absolutely. I've searched right into the yard. I've even had a walk round the town. And remember." Her chin quivered. "He… he ran away from somewhere before."

I looked at my watch. "Ten o'clock. Yes, that is strange. He shouldn't be out at this time."

As I spoke, the front door bell jangled. I galloped down the stairs and as I rounded the corner in the passage I could see Mrs. Heslington, the vicar's wife, through the glass. I threw open the door. She was holding Oscar in her arms.

"I believe this is your cat, Mr. Herriot," she said.

"It is indeed, Mrs. Heslington. Where did you find him?"

She smiled. "Well it was rather odd. We were having a meeting of the Mothers' Union at the church house and we noticed the cat just sitting there in the room."

Just sitting…?"

"Yes, as though he were listening to what we were saying and enjoying it all. It was unusual. When the meeting ended I thought I'd better bring him along to you."

"I'm most grateful, Mrs. Heslington." I snatched Oscar and tucked him under my arm. "My wife is distraught—she thought he was lost."

1. Supporting Facts:_______________________________________

____

Conclusion: Oscar the cat survived the operation and did not die.

2. Supporting Facts:_______________________________________

____

Conclusion: The cat was hiding in the garden.

3. Supporting Facts:_______________________________________

____

Conclusion: The narrator's wife thought the cat had run away.

Part II

Below is a passage from "The Egyptian Cinderella," by Shirley Climo.
Read the passage and then answer the questions that follow.

> Like the Egyptian servant girls, Rhodopis went to the water's edge each day to wash clothes or to gather the reeds that grew along the riverbank. But Rhodopis looked different from the Egyptian girls. Their eyes were brown and hers were green. Their hair hung straight to their shoulders, while the breeze blew hers into tangles. Their skin glowed like copper, but her pale skin burned red beneath the sun. That was how she got her name, for Rhodopis meant "rosy-cheeked" in Greek.
>
> "Rosy Rhodopis!" scoffed the servant girls, hissing her name between their teeth.
>
> Rhodopis pretended not to hear, but she blushed rosier than ever.

1. What conclusions can you draw about how Rhodopis felt living
   in Egypt?

   ____

   ____

2. List three facts from this passage that support the conclusion you
   have drawn.

   a. _______________________________________

   ____

   ____

   b. _______________________________________

   ____

   ____

   c. _______________________________________

   ____

   ____

3. List one conclusion you have drawn about the character of the other
   servant girls with whom Rhodopis had to work.

   ____

   ____

   ____

4. Give one supporting fact from the reading that supports your conclusion.

   ____

   ____

   ____

NAME _______________________________________   **DATE** _____________

Part III

Below is another passage from "The Egyptian Cinderella," by Shirley
Climo. Read the passage and answer the questions that follow.

> The servant girls gawked openmouthed as the Pharaoh kneeled before
> Rhodopis. He slipped the tiny shoe on her foot with ease. Then Rhodopis
> pulled its mate from the folds of her tunic.
>
> "Behold!" cried Amasis. "In all this land there is none so fit to
> be queen!"
>
> "But Rhodopis is a slave!" protested one of the servant girls.
>
> Kipa sniffed. "She is not even Egyptian."
>
> "She is the most Egyptian of all," the Pharaoh declared. "For her eyes
> are as green as the Nile, her hair as feathery as papyrus, and her skin the
> pink of a lotus flower."
>
> The Pharaoh led Rhodopis to the royal barge, and with every step, her
> rose-red slippers winked and sparkled in the sun.

Give one conclusion you have drawn from this passage about each of the
following characters. Under the conclusion, give one supporting fact that
backs it up. The first conclusion is filled in for you.

1. The Servant Girls
   Conclusion: The servant girls were jealous of Rhodopis.

   Supporting Fact: ____

   ____

2. Rhodopis
   Conclusion: ____

   Supporting Fact: ____

   ____

3. Amasis
   Conclusion: ____

   Supporting Fact: ____

   ____

Challenge!

How would you have to change the facts in this passage so that the
reader would come to the following conclusion?

   Conclusion: The servant girls loved Rhodopis and were happy about
what finally happened to her.

   Make up a supporting fact that might bring a reader to this conclusion:

____

____

SUMMARIZE

Introduction

To **summarize** means to tell briefly in your own words the main ideas of a piece of writing. When you summarize, you can condense your ideas or those of the writer into precise statements and omit unimportant details. When you are reading, you can choose and remember the most important parts of an author's writing. When readers write or tell the "short version" of what they have read, they summarize it. A summary includes the author's main ideas, but leaves out the supporting details.

Model

Read the following passage from "Mummy No. 1770," by Patricia Lauber. Find the main ideas and supporting details, think about how you would summarize this passage, and compare your ideas to the summary given below:

> Museums have a limited number of mummies. Each time one is unwrapped, the number grows smaller, and so autopsies are not often performed. But sometimes a museum has a mummy that is not important to its collections. This is a mummy that it does not want to display and a mummy about which almost nothing is known. As it happened, the Manchester Museum had just such a mummy. Its wrappings were in poor condition and no one knew what period it dated from, where it was found, or who the dead person was. The mummy was known only by its museum number, 1770. This was the mummy the museum made available to scientists who wanted to use modern techniques to study the wrappings and body in detail.

Here is a *summary* of the same passage:

The Manchester Museum had a mummy that was not important to its collection. The museum allowed scientists to unwrap and study it.

Practice

Read the following paragraph from "Mummy No. 1770," by Patricia Lauber, and answer the questions that follow:

When the Manchester team unwrapped the legs of Mummy 1770, they found, as the x-rays had shown, that both legs had been amputated, the left below the knee and the right above the knee. The mummy's right leg had been lengthened with a piece of wood to make it the same length as the left. The wood had been splinted to the leg bone. This meant there could not have been much, if any, flesh on the bone when the splinting was done. The feet were artificial and had gold toenail covers. The right foot was made of reeds and mud, with the ends of the reeds serving as toes. The left foot was simply a mass of reeds and mud.

1. What is the main idea of this paragraph?

____

2. Name three details that give more information about the main idea.

____

____

3. Use a complete sentence or sentences to summarize the paragraph.

____

____

4. **Challenge!**
   Read the following paragraph and write a summary of one or
   two sentences.

In other ways, Mummy 1770 was both interesting and puzzling. The evidence indicated that the body had been in a state of considerable decay when the embalmers worked on it. The wooden leg was attached to bone. All the internal organs were missing and so was the left kneecap, which suggested that the ligaments holding it in place had rotted away. The red and blue paint on the skull bones was a sign that the hair and scalp had been missing.

Summary

____

____

____

____

____

____

PARAPHRASE

Introduction

When you use your own words to repeat someone else's message, you **paraphrase** what they have said. Paraphrasing is a helpful reading tool. When you are reading, identify the main ideas and their supporting details. If you can retell a story accurately in your own words, it shows that you understand the meaning of what you have read. Unlike a summary, where the reader is concerned mostly with the author's main ideas, a paraphrase also includes details.

Model

Read this passage from "Beware of the Dog," by Roald Dahl. Paraphrase it in your mind as you read it. Compare your paraphrase with the one below.

> Down below there was only a vast white undulating sea of cloud. Above there was the sun and the sun was white like the clouds, because it is never yellow when one looks at it from high in the air.
>
> He was still flying the Spitfire. His right hand was on the stick and he was working the rudder-bar with his left leg alone. It was quite easy. The machine was flying well. He knew what he was doing.
>
> Everything is fine, he thought. I'm doing all right. I'm doing nicely. I know my way home. I'll be there in half an hour. When I land I shall taxi in and switch off my engine and I shall say, help me to get out, will you. I shall make my voice sound ordinary and natural and none of them will take any notice. Then I shall say, someone help me get out. I can't do it alone because I've lost one of my legs. They'll all laugh and think that I'm joking.

Paraphrased Version

The author is flying a plane and feeling confident about his aircraft and his abilities as a pilot. When he lands and switches off the engine he plans to ask for help in leaving the cockpit because he has only one leg. He imagines that everyone will think he's joking.

Practice

Paraphrase the following passage from "Beware of the Dog," by Roald Dahl.

> He saw a small house with a gray tiled roof standing alone beside a narrow lane, and immediately behind it there was a plowed field. In front of the house there was an untidy garden, and there was a green hedge separating the garden from the lane. He was looking at the hedge when he saw the sign. It was just a piece of board nailed to the top of a short pole, and because the hedge had not been trimmed for a long time, the branches had grown out around the sign so that it seemed almost as though it had been placed in the middle of the hedge. There was something written on the board with white paint. He pressed his head against the glass of the window, trying to read what it said.

____

____

____

____

____

____

____

____

Application
STRATEGY

FORM GENERALIZATIONS

Introduction

Effective readers sometimes act as detectives. They look for specific clues in their reading material and put these clues together to solve the mystery of the larger meaning of what they have read. When readers do this, they form **generalizations**, or broad ideas on what might be true in the book, story, or passage. To form generalizations as you read, look carefully for sentences that relate to each other. Then ask yourself if the sentences give you general information that might be true, but not directly stated. If so, you have formed a generalization.

Model

Read the following passage from "Eugenie Clark and the Sleeping Sharks," by Margery Facklam. As you read, try to form one or more generalizations about the information in the passage. See if your generalizations agree with the example given below.

> Three reef whitetip sharks lived in a tank at the laboratory, and they ate anything dropped into the water. One day as Eugenie was experimenting with the fish, she found one small Moses sole that had not been completely "milked" of its poison. She put a string through its gills, which did not hurt it, and lowered the fish into the sharks' tank. The moment the sole touched the water, the sharks swept toward it with mouths open wide. But when they got within a few feet of the fish on the string, the sharks' jaws seemed to be frozen open. They dashed away, shaking their heads as though trying to get rid of something awful. For six hours, Eugenie watched the sharks approach the sole, and the reactions were the same each time the sharks swam near the poisonous fish.

Generalization
- Sharks have some kind of natural mechanism that warns them not to eat things that are poisonous.

This sentence states the central idea of the paragraph.

Supporting information from the passage
- The sharks would normally eat anything dropped into their tank.
- The sharks opened their mouths to swallow the fish at first.
- Something made them stay away from the poisonous fish.
- They had the same reaction for six hours.

This supporting information helps to illustrate the generalization.

NAME _________________________________   DATE ___________

Practice

Read these two passages from "Eugenie Clark and the Sleeping Sharks," by Margery Facklam. Make at least one generalization about each passage, and support it with information found there.

> A stockaded pen, forty by seventy feet, was built next to the dock to hold the live sharks. A tiger shark, named Hazel, and a reddish color nurse shark, named Rosy, were two of the first guests in the pen, and a new problem arose. Nosy visitors, ignoring signs and fences, poked around and teased the animals. Eugenie was worried that both people and sharks would be hurt. When several of the sharks were killed by trespassers, Eugenie began to talk to groups in the community, especially at schools. She explained what sharks eat and how they live. Whenever people know about an animal, they fear it less. Soon the newspapers labeled her the "shark lady." It is a name that has stayed with her in spite of all her research with other sea creatures.

1. Generalization(s)

____

____

2. Supporting Information

____

____

> Eugenie discovered fresh water seeping into the caves, diluting the sea water. There was less salt in the caves than in the open ocean. She remembered that when she was a kid she would put her saltwater fish into fresh water for a little while so that the parasites would drop off. Perhaps the same thing was happening with the sharks. Maybe these eighteen-foot tiger and reef sharks were intelligent enough to seek comfort in the caves.
>
> Eugenie had taught sharks to ring a bell and push targets for meals and to distinguish right from wrong targets at the Florida laboratory. "Surely," she said, "they are capable of learning that in water of below-normal salinity, a condition they apparently must sense, annoying parasites loosen their grip."

1. Generalization(s)

____

____

2. Supporting Information

____

____

NAME ____   **DATE** ______________

Read the following passage. Then answer the questions that follow. Write the letter of the correct answer on the line at the right.

> Deluded by his reflection, Narcissus fell in love with the beauty that was his own. Without thought of food or rest he lay beside the pool addressing cries and pleas to the image, whose lips moved as he spoke but whose reply he could never catch. Echo came by, the most constant of disdained lovers. She was a nymph who had once angered Hera, the wife of Zeus, by talking too much, and in consequence was deprived of the use of her tongue for ordinary conversations: all she could do was repeat the last words of others. Seeing Narcissus lying there, she pleaded with him in his own words. "I will die unless you pity me," cried Narcissus to his beloved. "Pity me," cried Echo as vainly to hers.

1. Which statement best expresses the main idea of the passage?   1. ______
   A. Narcissus and Echo are in love with each other.
   B. Narcissus and Echo each love in vain.
   C. It is important to love others more than oneself.
   D. Echo is committed to love Narcissus forever.

2. According to the selection, what caused Echo to lose the capacity for ordinary   2. ______
   conversation?
   A. She could only repeat the last words of others.
   B. She fell in love with Narcissus.
   C. She angered Hera, who deprived her of the use of her tongue.
   D. Narcissus thought she talked too much.

Read the following passage. Then answer the questions that follow. Write the letter of the correct answer on the line at the right.

> "Where ya goin', Froggy?" he shouted, even though it was perfectly obvious—I was taking the usual shortcut across the pizza place's parking lot, to the Shop-Rite. What he wasn't going to understand was why I wasn't going *into* the supermarket, but around back. They throw pretty fair stuff out there, the beat-up vegetables and bread and such that not even charity groups want. You can pick up quite a bit if you get there before the bag ladies do.
>
> I didn't answer Jerry back, so when I went around to the dumpsters, naturally he came after me. He sounded a little worried. "Froggo? Whatcha doin'?"

3. Which statement expresses the implied main idea of the passage?   3. ______
   A. Froggy often uses the back entrance to the supermarket.
   B. Froggy does not want to be seen ordering a pizza.
   C. Froggy is hoping to receive food from charity groups.
   D. Froggy is going to gather food from the dumpsters and does not want
      anyone to see him do it.

4. Read the sentence. Then choose the meaning of the underlined word. Write   4. _______
the letter of the correct answer on the line at the right.

Arleen went to tell the neighbors that their goat had eaten most of the plants in
her mother's garden, and the chilly greeting they gave her was not very <u>hospitable</u>.

   A. negative   **C.** welcoming
   B. like a hospital   **D.** hostile

5. Read the sentence. Then choose the meaning of the underlined word. Write   5. _______
the letter of the correct answer on the line on the right.

A little like a stuck machine, Frank sat there <u>compulsively</u> picking at the buttons
on his shirt while the principal scolded him.

   A. unable to stop   **C.** sleepily
   B. happily   **D.** without fear

6. Read the sentence. Then choose the meaning of the underlined word. Write   6. _______
the letter of the correct answer on the line at the right.

The earthquake shook the huge building in a way that seemed <u>inconceivable</u> to
Clara, like a dog shaking an old rag in its teeth.

   A. through a sieve   **C.** weak
   B. very calm   **D.** unthinkable

Read the following passage. Then answer the questions that follow. Write the letter
of the correct answer on the line at the right.

"This is a kind horse, a gentle and a faithful horse," Pierre said, "and I can see a
beautiful spirit shining out of the eyes of the horse. I will name him after good
St. Joseph, who was also kind and gentle and faithful and a beautiful spirit."

Within a year Joseph knew the milk route as well as Pierre. Pierre used to boast
that he didn't need reins—he never touched them. Each morning Pierre arrived
at the stables of the Provençal Milk Company at five o'clock. The wagon would
be loaded and Joseph hitched to it. Pierre would call *"Bon jour, vieille ami,"*[1] as
he climbed into his seat and Joseph would turn his head and the other drivers
would smile and say that the horse would smile at Pierre. Then Jacques, the
foreman, would say, "All right Pierre, go on," and Pierre would call softly to
Joseph, *"Avance, mon ami,"*[2] and this splendid combination would stalk proudly
down the street.

---
1. *Bon jour, vieille ami:* Good morning, old friend."
2. *Avance, mon ami:* "Forward, my friend."

7. According to the selection, why did Pierre name the horse Joseph?   7. _______
   A. because his favorite son's name was Joseph
   B. because the horse's beautiful spirit reminded him of St. Joseph
   C. because St. Joseph is the patron saint of horses
   D. because a horse he had owned before was called Joseph

8. Which word rhymes with the word *reins*?   8. ______
   A. rhymes
   B. rings
   C. trains
   D. seems

9. Which word rhymes with the word *rough*?   9. ______
   A. so
   B. puff
   C. row
   D. dough

10. When Pierre arrived at the Provençal Milk Company each morning, what had   10. ______
    already been done?
    A. He had already eaten lunch.
    B. The milk had already been delivered.
    C. The wagon would be loaded and Joseph hitched to it.
    D. The foreman had sent the other drivers out.

11. Choose the word that rhymes with the first syllable in *beau-ti-ful*.   11. ______
    A. bow
    B. teen
    C. new
    D. loan

Read the sentence. Then answer the question that follows. Write the letter of the
correct answer on the line at the right.

Graduation day is a _______________ that most students look forward to for years.

12. Choose the word that best fills the blank.   12. ______
    A. right
    B. wright
    C. rite
    D. right

Read the following passages. Then answer the questions that follow. Write the
letter of the correct answer on the line at the right.

Our galaxy, the Milky Way, has its stars arranged on arms that curve out from the
center bulge. It is a type we call a spiral galaxy. One of our neighbors in space,
the Andromeda Galaxy, is another spiral. In fact, spirals are very common in the
universe. But they are not all alike. In some spiral galaxies, the arms are much
closer together than in our own galaxy. In others, the arms are more wide open.

Another type of spiral galaxy is very different. It has the spiral arms coming
from a band of stars that passes through the center. We call this type a barred-
spiral galaxy.

Some galaxies have no arms at all. They are either round or oval in shape and
are known as ellipticals.

NAME ___________________________________ **DATE** ___________

13. What are the three main types of galaxies?
    A. Milky Way, center bulge, and spiral
    B. spiral, barred-spiral, and elliptical
    C. closed spiral, open spiral, and no spiral
    D. Milky Way, Andromeda, and no arms

13. ______

> The Earth also has another motion in relation to the sun. It orbits, or circles, around the sun once every $365\frac{1}{4}$ days, the period we call a year. It orbits in this way because it is a planet, held in its place by the sun's powerful gravity. The sun also holds captive eight other planets. They orbit the sun in the following times: Mercury 88 days, Venus 225 days, Mars 687 days, Jupiter 11.9 years, Saturn 29.5 years, Uranus 84 years, Neptune 165 years, Pluto 248 years.
>
> Compared with the other bodies, the sun is huge. It contains 750 times more mass than all of them put together. Its diameter, about 865,000 miles, is 100 times larger than the Earth's.

14. Which planets take more than a year to orbit the sun?
    A. Jupiter, Uranus, Neptune, Venus, and Pluto
    B. Mercury, Venus, Mars, Jupiter, and Saturn
    C. Earth, Mars, Jupiter, and Neptune
    D. Mars, Jupiter, Uranus, Neptune, and Pluto

14. ______

15. How does the orbiting time of Mars compare with that of Earth?
    A. They are almost exactly the same.
    B. Earth's is almost twice that of Mars.
    C. Earth's is a little more than half that of Mars.
    D. Mars' orbit is more than twice that of Earth.

15. ______

16. How does the size of the sun contrast with that of the planets?
    A. Its mass is 100 times that of Earth.
    B. It has 750 times the mass of all of them put together.
    C. The Sun is made of flames, which have no dimensions or weight.
    D. The Sun's diameter is 865,000 miles more than that of the other planets.

16. ______

17. Some information in the selection is important and some is unimportant. Which information is unimportant?
    A. A period of $365\frac{1}{4}$ days is called a year.
    B. The sun is the center of the solar system.
    C. Jupiter, Saturn, Uranus, Neptune, and Pluto take many years to circle the sun.
    D. The sun holds all the planets captive through gravity.

17. ______

18. How should the word *gravity* be divided into syllables?
    A. grav-i-ty
    B. gra-vi-ty
    C. gravi-ty
    D. gra-vit-y

18. ______

NAME _______________________________   **DATE** _______________

19. How should the word *diameter* be divided into syllables?   19. ______
   A. dia-met-er
   B. di-am-et-er
   C. di-am-e-ter
   D. dia-met-er

Read the sentences. Then answer the questions that follow. Write the letter of the correct answer on the line at the right.

The story contained few remarkable facts. A factory in which satisfactory water tanks were manufactured was forced to close. One factor was the less than factual bookkeeping. The dissatisfaction of the company factotums also had to be factored into the failure.

20. Many words in the selection contain the word root *fact*. It comes from the   20. ______
   Latin verb *facere*. What verb best defines the meaning of *fact* in these words?
   A. to fake
   B. to fail
   C. to make or do
   D. to cheat

21. What does the prefix *pro-* mean in the word *proclaim*?   21. ______
   A. away
   B. before
   C. from
   D. again

22. What does the suffix *-claim* mean in the word *proclaim*?   22. ______
   A. extremely
   B. claim a loss
   C. cry out
   D. many times

Read the following passages. Then answer the questions that follow. Write the letter of the correct answer on the line at the right.

Anyone thinking about numbers must come to the conclusion that there are a great many of them and feel at a loss to express just how many. In poetry, one could make use of some simile: "as many as the sands of the sea"; "as numerous as the stars that shine and twinkle in the Milky Way."

To the mathematician, however, similes are of no use. To him, it merely seems that the integers are formed by beginning with one, adding one to that for the next number, and one to that for the next number, and so on. Since the mathematical rules do not set any limits to addition (*any* two numbers may be added) there can be no end to this process. After all, however large a number is named—*however large*—though it stretch in a line of small figures from here to the farthest star, it is always possible to say "that number plus one" and have a still higher number.

NAME ____   DATE _______________

23. Which of the following statements is a *fact* presented in the selection?   23. ______
    A. Integers are formed by beginning with two numbers.
    B. Mathematical rules do not set any limits to addition.
    C. No two numbers may be added.
    D. Mathematicians do not like similes.

A Fox once saw a Crow fly off with a piece of cheese in its beak and settle on a branch of a tree. "That's for me, as I am a Fox," said Master Reynard, and he walked up to the foot of a tree.

"Good day, Mistress Crow," he cried. "How well you are looking today: how glossy your feathers; how bright your eye. I feel sure your voice must surpass that of other birds, just as your figure does; let me hear but one song from you that I may greet you as the Queen of the Birds."

The Crow lifted up her head and began to caw her best, but the moment she opened her mouth the piece of cheese fell to the ground, only to be snapped up by Master Fox. "That will do," said he. "That was all I wanted. In exchange for your cheese I will give you a piece of advice for the future—

"Do not trust flatterers."

24. Which of the following is an *opinion* presented in the selection?   24. ______
    A. Crow's voice could surpass that of other birds.
    B. Fox wanted Crow's piece of cheese.
    C. Crow could not sing.
    D. Crow's voice could not surpass that of other birds.

25. Which of the following best describes the author's purpose in writing   25. ______
the selection?
    A. to show readers how unfair it is to trick someone
    B. to point out how strange it would be for a crow to eat cheese
    C. to prove that having a beautiful voice isn't important
    D. to amuse readers with a story of how a clever fox used flattery to fool a
       vain crow

Read the following passage. Then answer the question that follows. Write the letter of the correct answer on the line at the right.

Mama and Aunt Margot used to whisper about how Grandpa was losing his mind. Every night, as they scraped the grease off the black pans in the kitchen, they would tell lies about him. Well, it was true that sometimes he still talked to Grandma as he rocked back and forth on the dark porch. Once in a while, I would hide behind the door to listen to him tell her about the family and about their old friends, and he would even ask her questions. It scared me. Because you see, Grandma was dead and he still talked to her. But that doesn't mean he was crazy, does it?

26. Which of the following best describes the author's point of view toward Grandpa? **26.** ______
  A. The author thinks that Grandpa is insane.
  B. The author thinks Grandpa is normal, but that Mama and Aunt Margot are making up false stories about him.
  C. The author thinks Grandpa is old and a little strange, but not really crazy.
  D. The author thinks Grandpa is normal, but that everyone else is insane.

Read the following passage. Then answer the question that follows. Write the letter of the correct answer on the line at the right.

That night the wind swept over and around the tent in its hole on the high ridge of the mountain. Tomorrow they would attempt the most dangerous part of the climb. As they tried to rest, each man had his own thoughts. Dana wondered what Ned and Sharon were doing and where the rest of the team was on the mountain. Doug thought about his wife, Barbara, whom he missed so much. Would he see her again? For a moment he wondered, and then he brushed aside the disturbing thought. As the wind clawed at their tent, it seemed as if the mountain were alive and jealous of its lofty, solitary majesty.

27. Which of the following would be the best conclusion about what Dana and Doug are facing? **27.** ______
  A. They are trying to win promotions to higher paying jobs.
  B. They are part of a movie-making crew in Hollywood.
  C. They have been separated from friends and family by a record-breaking blizzard.
  D. They are camped on the side of a mountain during a difficult and dangerous climb.

Use the chart below to answer the following questions.

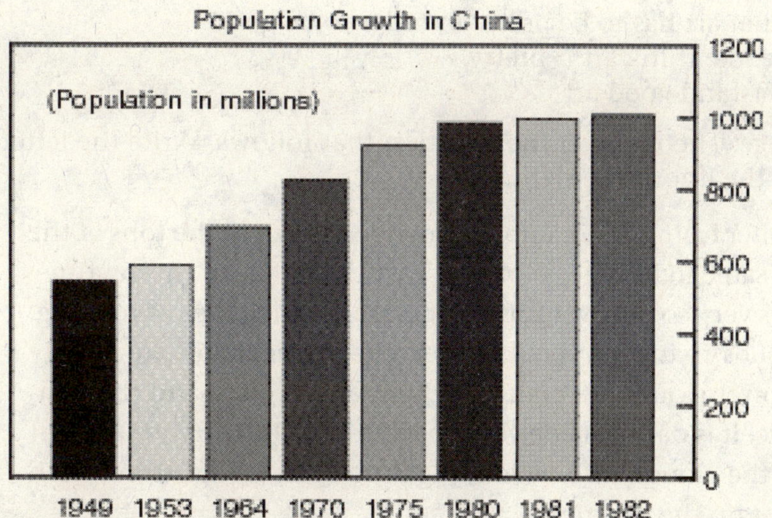

28. What is the earliest year shown in the bar graph? **28.** ______
  A. 1949
  B. 1953
  C. 1994
  D. 1982

NAME ____   DATE ____________

29. What was the population of China in 1953?   29. _______
    A. 588
    B. 695,000,000
    C. 588,000,000
    D. 588,000

Read the following passage. Then answer the question that follows. Write the letter of the correct answer on the line at the right.

From the first, the local Chinese were not Jade Snow's patrons. The thinness and whiteness of porcelains imported from China and ornate decorations which came into vogue during the late Ching Dynasty[1] satisfied their tastes. They could not understand why "silly Americans" paid dollars for a hand-thrown bowl[2] utilizing crude California colored clays, not much different from the inexpensive peasant ware of China. That the Jade Snow Wong bowl went back to an older tradition of understated beauty was not apparent. They could see only that she wouldn't apply a dragon or a hundred flowers.

    Many years later when Jade Snow met another atypical artist, a scholar and calligrapher[3] born and educated in China, he was to say to her, "I shudder if the majority of people look at my brush work and say it is pretty, for then I know it is ordinary and I have failed. If they say they do not understand it, or even that it is ugly, I am happy, for I have succeeded."

1. **Ching Dynasty:** This dynasty lasted from 1644 to 1912.
2. **hand-thrown bowl:** A bowl shaped by hand on a potter's wheel.
3. **calligrapher** (kəh lig′ rəh fər) *n.*: Someone skilled in the art of beautiful handwriting.

30. Which of the following statements best summarizes the passage?   30. _______
    A. The artist thinks that a successful work of art does not have to be pretty.
    B. The artist thinks that art has to be pretty in order to be good.
    C. The majority of people think art is pretty.
    D. People never understand good art.

Read the following passage. Then answer the question that follows. Write the letter of the correct answer on the line at the right.

Imagine exploring Jupiter from a spaceship. As you look down at the tops of the clouds, the air has the same light blue color that Earth's sky has in the daytime. The temperature here is very cold—over 250 degrees (Fahrenheit) below freezing.

    The colors of the clouds change as you fly lower. The upper clouds are mainly white and blue. The lower clouds are orange, yellow, and brown, and the temperature is warmer here. It is dark outside your spaceship, as little or no sunlight filters down through the clouds. Below you, gigantic bolts of lightning flash across the sky and light up the darkness.

    Jupiter's "surface" is an ocean of liquid hydrogen that covers the entire planet. This ocean may be ten thousand or more miles deep—no one knows. Perhaps Jupiter has no solid surface at all but is entirely liquid down to its rocky center, almost nine thousand miles below the clouds.

31. Choose the statement that is the best generalization about the composition of   **31.** ______
the planet Jupiter.
  A. Jupiter has a very thick atmosphere, but may have no solid surface.
  B. Jupiter's atmosphere is made of liquid hydrogen, much like Earth's oceans.
  C. Jupiter's atmosphere is blue, like Earth's, but its ocean is orange, yellow,
and brown.
  D. Jupiter has no real atmosphere and its ocean is made of liquid rocks.

Read the following passage. Then answer the question that follows. Write the letter
of the correct answer on the line at the right.

> She raised her face, and I knew what she wanted me to do. I bent and brushed
> my lips against her cheek. Her flesh was like a leaf in autumn, crisp and dry.

32. Which of the following best paraphrases the passage?   **32.** ______
  A. When she lifted her face I knew she wanted me to kiss her. I leaned down
and kissed her cheek. Her skin was dry.
  B. She raised her face, and I knew what she wanted me to do. I bent and brushed
my lips against her cheek. Her flesh was like a leaf in autumn, crisp and dry.
  C. She lifted her face up and I kissed her.
  D. I didn't want to kiss her face because her skin was dry.